ds of Pennsylvania

tto M. Vondrak - Not an official map. Not all lines and locations shown.

RAILROADS of
PENNSYLVANIA

Your Guide To Pennsylvania's Historic Trains and Railway Sites

Brian Solomon

Voyageur Press

Dedication

To my brother, Seán

First published in 2008 by Voyageur Press, an imprint of MBI Publishing Company, 400 First Avenue North, Suite 300, Minneapolis, MN 55401 USA

Voyageur Press titles are also available at discounts in bulk quantity for industrial or sales-promotional use. For details write to Special Sales Manager at MBI Publishing Company, 400 First Avenue North, Suite 300, Minneapolis, MN 55401 USA.

To find out more about our books, join us online at www.voyageurpress.com.

ISBN-13: 978-0-7603-3245-0

Editor: Leah Noel
Designer: LeAnn Kuhlmann

Printed in China

Library of Congress Cataloging-in-Publication Data

Solomon, Brian.
  Railroads of Pennsylvania : your guide to Pennsylvania's historic trains and railway sites /
  By Brian Solomon.
    p. cm.
  ISBN-13: 978-0-7603-3245-0 (hardbound w/ jacket)
  ISBN-10: 0-7603-3245-2 (hardbound w/ jacket)
  1. Railroads--Pennsylvania--History. I. Title.
TF24.P4S65 2008
385.09748--dc22

                    2007046261

On the frontispiece: Electro-Motive's model E7 was a mass-produced streamlined diesel-electric designed for long-distance passenger service. It was among several model types to use the classic "bull dog nose" introduced in 1939 on the FT freight diesel. PRR 5901, built in 1945 and classed by the railroad as an EP20, is the last surviving E7A. It is preserved at the Railroad Museum of Pennsylvania, where it is displayed along with other classic steam, diesel, and electric locomotives. *Brian Solomon*

On the title page: Strasburg Rail Road No. 90 takes water after its late afternoon run to and from Leaman's Place. A set of vintage wooden-heathed passengers bask in the glow of a summer sun. *Brian Solomon*

Facing page, top: The Wanamaker, Kempton & Southern is a joy for visitors of all ages. The thrill of a live steam locomotive and the opportunity to ride a real caboose is difficult to resist. A summer Sunday at Kempton has all the visitors enthralled with the spirit of railroading. *Brian Solomon*

Facing page, bottom: Pennsylvania Railroad was known for its multiple-arch masonry viaducts. Among the most massive is the so-called Big Viaduct, east of Mineral Point on the west slope near Johnstown. Built to carry four tracks, this bridge is unusual because of its size and its construction on a curve. On a clear April morning, Amtrak's *Pennsylvanian* climbs eastward across the famous bridge. This location is accessible by a healthy walk along an old right-of-way that is east of Mineral Point toward South Fork. The bridge is only a few miles from the famous Staple Bend Tunnel, located on the right-of-way of the old Portage Railroad. *Brian Solomon*

On the contents page: A red sunrise at J Tower. Built in 1884, this classic Victorian switch tower served for 99 years before being preserved on the Strasburg Rail Road. Towers were railroad nerve centers where highly trained signalmen, levermen, and operators governed movements over the line to maximize railroad efficiency while ensuring a high level of safety. *Brian Solomon*

On the acknowledgments page: Although it was once commonplace across Pennsylvania, the sight of a steam-powered freight had effectively vanished from the landscape by 1960. Nostalgia for steam resulted in the creation of tourist lines, such as the Strasburg Rail Road, which have preserved steam locomotives and used them to recreate scenes such as this with former Norfolk and Western 4-8-0 No. 475 on February 18, 2006. *Chris Bost*

On the foreword page: The view from the 1891 railroad station at New Hope finds Baldwin 2-8-0 in steam on the platform. New Hope & Ivyland provides an atmosphere of classic railroading, while also serving as a freight-hauling short line to serve customers along its line. *Brian Solomon*

On the foreword page, inset: Pennsylvania Railroad's GG1 electric is among the most famous mid-twentieth-century American locomotives. Designed by the railroad for high-speed passenger service, it was styled by pioneer industrial designer Raymond Loewy, who suggested a welded skin and added the characteristic pinstripes. No. 4935 survived into the Amtrak era, was restored to its original appearance in the late 1970s, and was repainted again in the 1980s for display at the Railroad Museum of Pennsylvania. *Brian Solomon*

CONTENTS

ACKNOWLEDGMENTS

My earliest experiences in Pennsylvania were through childhood visits with my family. I'll never forget my first thrilling minutes at Horseshoe Curve. I leapt the stairs to watch the passing of an SD45 and then inspected the K4s Pacific that was still displayed at the park. Since that time, I've made numerous visits to see Pennsylvania's railroads, and my enthusiasm for them has never waned. In writing and creating photographs for this book, my familiarity with Pennsylvania and its railroads guided my efforts. Yet, along the way, I owe many thanks to the people who helped me.

Over the years, Tom S. Hoover and I have shared numerous adventures exploring old Pennsylvania railroads. We made week-long trips in the 1980s and 1990s, as well as more recent excursions to perfect our photography. Tom's family has hosted me in Pennsylvania for more than 20 years. His father, Tom

M. Hoover, and I have explored the East Broad Top to observe its preserved operation and to seek out the remnants of its disused lines. Over the last decade, Michael L. Gardner and I explored lines across the state to seek out obscure coal routes, to look for interesting photographic angles, and to absorb the atmosphere. Since our early days, my brother Seán and I have made many trips in Pennsylvania. In recent years, we've explored lines near Seán's home in Philadelphia. Most recently, as this book was in final production, my brother and Isabel Dijols led a canoe trip along the Schuylkill to inspect and photograph railroad bridges. Tim Doherty and I made trips to see the Starrucca Viaduct and the Tunkhannock Viaduct, and we followed along the old Northern Central/P&E routes to photograph Juniata Terminal's PRR E units and Norfolk Southern coal trains.

The research for this book included using my experiences and notes, while consulting dozens of books, hundreds of magazines, and countless documents. Along every step of the way, knowledgeable people assisted my efforts. Those who were especially helpful include John Gruber, who provided me with contacts, source material, and who wrote portions of the text, and John P. Hankey, a historian and friend who directed my focus, introduced me to fellow historians, and assisted with my understanding of Pennsylvania's role in American railroad development. Special thanks to Kurt Bell and David Dunn at the Railroad Museum of Pennsylvania for access to the museum and its extensive archives. In addition, Kurt hosted me at the Strasburg Rail Road and provided a detailed history of it for this book. Thanks to Andrew R. Ottinger for his help on the Middletown & Hummelstown.

Steamtown's archivist and historian, Patrick McKnight, helped me navigate the extensive Steamtown archive and library, located engineering drawings of Tunkhannock and Martins Creek viaducts, provided detailed literature on the Steamtown collection, and gave walking tours of the grounds, including the Mattes Street signal tower. Thanks to Scott Snell for slide shows in Easton and for photographs of eastern Pennsylvania. John Hartman and George Legler of the Wanamaker, Kempton & Southern entertained my photographic trips to that line. Thanks also to Chris Bost for his help. Bryant Schmude provided a tour and background materials at the Pennsylvania Trolley Museum.

Patrick Yough assisted in many ways. In addition to providing text on the B&LE, he gave tours of railways in the Pittsburgh area and in the Delaware River Valley, granted access to his library, supplied photography, and helped with proofing text, tracking down facts, and making introductions. William S. Young provided valuable insight and information on the Starrucca and Tunkhannock viaducts. Will Holloway and Brad Hellman accompanied me on tours of B&O's Sand Patch grade. Mark Leppert provided tours of PRR's legendary grade. Thanks also to Clark Johnson for a trip across Pennsylvania on the private car *Caritas*, including a twilight ride around Horseshoe Curve.

The Irish Railway Record Society in Dublin allowed me unrestricted access to its archives and assisted in locating rare and unusual documents relating to both Pennsylvania's railways and early British-built locomotives. Doug Eisele made trips on the Delaware-Lackawanna Railroad possible—likewise, thanks to DL's crews and dispatchers. A variety of photographers lent me their fine work to help illustrate this book; each is credited appropriately. Otto Vondrak provided the custom-drawn map.

My father has been photographing Pennsylvania railways since the 1950s; his photography encouraged my interest and inspired our railroad-themed family trips. In addition to providing a wide selection of images for this project, giving me information on Philadelphia area railways, and lending me use of his extensive library, he proofread the text. My mother, Maureen, assisted with my complex travel logistics, international communication, and accounting. Special thanks to Dennis Pernu, Leah Noel, and everyone at Voyageur Press for taking a text and collected photos and transforming it into a book! I hope you enjoy reading it as much as I enjoyed writing it.

FOREWORD

Welcome to the world of Pennsylvania railroads. On your journey through this book, you will be treated to the sights and sounds of Keystone State railroads, both past and present, which range from the main line rounding Horseshoe Curve near Altoona to a pastoral branch line at the Wanamaker, Kempton & Southern in Kempton.

Through these pages, author Brian Solomon traces the strong ties between the railroad and industry in Pennsylvania, beginning with the opening of the Mauch Chunk Gravity Railroad in 1827. As the main source for much of the nation's coal in the nineteenth and twentieth century, Pennsylvania quickly became a railroad state—at one time it was home to thousands of miles of railway trackage that helped transport both freight and passengers across the country.

Many of these lines were owned or controlled by the Pennsylvania Railroad, one of the most profitable and heavily used railroads of its time. Organized in 1846, the company represented a consolidation of more than 600 smaller lines, extending from its Philadelphia headquarters to New York, Washington D.C., Chicago, and St. Louis. Numerous major commercial and passenger railroads also had lines running through the Keystone State—the Baltimore & Ohio; The Erie Railroad; Delaware, Lackawanna & Western; the Reading Company; the Bessemer & Lake Erie (serving the steel industry); the Lehigh Valley; Nickel Plate Road; and even parts of Pennsylvania's archrival, the New York Central. Many smaller lines sprang up to connect small towns or were constructed specifically to tap mines, reach industries, or, as temporary lines, to haul timber harvests.

Eventually, Pennsylvania cities like Philadelphia, Reading, Pittsburgh, Scranton, and Harrisburg became hubs for the railroad. Thousands of Pennsylvanians earned their living working in the rail industry. Altoona, at the foot of the Allegheny crossing and on the edge of bituminous coal country, developed as PRR's primary shop town and as an important freight classification yard. Here, the Pennsylvania Railroad built hundreds of its own locomotives. In Philadelphia, the Baldwin Locomotive Works developed as the world's largest locomotive maker and turned out hundreds of machines each year.

Today, the commonwealth is still home to many freight and passenger lines, as well as preserved railways, museums, and sites. One hundred and thirty-six of Pennsylvania's railroads, stations, bridges, and tunnels are listed as either National Historic Landmarks or on the National Register of Historic Places. Among these are the Steamtown National Historic Site in Scranton, Altoona's Horseshoe Curve, and East Broad Top at Orbisonia, all of which are visited each year by thousands of rail enthusiasts wanting to relive a bygone era. This book is a guide to the best of Pennsylvania's rail sites, both past and present, to help you understand the Keystone State's unique role in American railroading. For a more general view of railroading's heritage, visit the Center for Railroad Photography & Art's internet archive, www.railroadheritage.org. It is rich with images of Pennsylvania and national interest, and the descriptive texts introduce many facets of railroad history illustrated in the images.

With this book as a guide, you can venture out across the commonwealth and enjoy its vast railroad resources. So, have a great time while searching out the best of Pennsylvania railroading.

—John Gruber, President, Center for Railroad
Photography & Art, Madison, Wisconsin

PART I
ANTHRACITE COUNTRY

Railroading got its beginning in the anthracite region of Pennsylvania. What began as an outgrowth of the canal movement soon developed into a business of its own. Anthracite propelled America's first industrial revolution, which fueled further railroad building. Parallel main lines were built as companies vied for movement of "black diamonds," more commonly known as coal.

By the late nineteenth century, eastern Pennsylvania's anthracite lines were some of the busiest and most intensely built railroads in the whole country. Anthracite mining peaked in the early decades of the twentieth century and then entered a long period of decline. This decline corresponded with tough times for the region's railroads. Large-scale consolidation and abandonment began in the 1950s, which was decades before similar retrenchment elsewhere in the commonwealth. By 1971, regular passenger services had ended on all lines in the region. Although many freight lines were abandoned or had their plants scaled back, the region remains rich with railroad heritage. A number of lines still carry freight on a daily basis. Today, this area is also home to several railroad museums, excursion railroads, and historic sites. The best known, and perhaps the most interesting, is Steamtown, which has preserved the heart of the old Delaware, Lackawanna & Western shops and yards at Scranton.

The Scranton/Wilkes-Barre region is still served by several active freight railroads. While the movement of anthracite is just a trickle compared to its glory days, freight is again on the rise. Long freight trains still use of some of the old anthracite railroad main lines—now run by different companies. Other lines have been adapted as rail-trails, or lay reclaimed by nature as remnants of an earlier era. A wealth of railroad heritage is here and waiting to be explored.

Alco's model RS3 was used by many railroads to replace aging steam locomotives in the mid-1950s. These locomotives were bought by the Delaware & Hudson. Now more than 50 years later, they are still earning revenue by hauling freight for Delaware-Lackawanna, a short line that serves both former Delaware & Hudson and Delaware, Lackawanna & Western trackage in the Scranton area. At the end of the day, DL RS3s 4103 and 4118 cross Bridge 60 in Scranton. Brian Solomon

CHAPTER 1

BLACK DIAMONDS AND THE GRAVITY RAILROAD

The rolling bucolic mountains of eastern Pennsylvania were blessed (or cursed) with one of the world's largest deposits of anthracite or hard coal—known to early settlers as stone coal. Once coal became a desirable source of fuel in the early nineteenth century, northeastern Pennsylvania's four anthracite fields between the Susquehanna and Delaware rivers were in high demand. The coal mined from these fields first moved along the rivers. It was shipped in crudely built boats known as flatbottom arcs that served a dual purpose of delivering timber and coal to urban consumers.

As the demand for anthracite increased, the burgeoning coal industry needed a more effective and economical means for transporting its product. By the mid-1820s, the growing flood of anthracite encouraged construction of an extensive, privately run canal network. By 1830, according to *The Kingdom of Coal*, an estimated 200,000 tons of hard coal was shipped annually to Philadelphia.

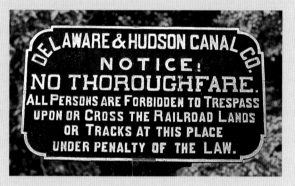

Mauch Chunk Gravity Railroad

Many of America's earliest commercial railways were conceived by canal companies to assist in transporting anthracite from the mines to canal heads. These primordial railways, like their counterparts in Britain, were specialized tram lines. They set precedents that encouraged later and more substantial railroad development, although these early lines were only conceptually related to the full-service railroads that developed in their wake.

Around 1825, industrialist and anthracite pioneer Josiah White envisioned a tram railway to connect the Lehigh coal mines at Summit Hill, Pennsylvania, with the growing anthracite transport hub at Mauch Chunk (today known as Jim Thorpe) on the Lehigh River. This railway was intended to augment the existing wagon road built a few years earlier for the same purpose. Although tram lines in collieries had existed for decades in Britain, most of these lines were very short and relied upon animal

Facing page: Although the old Mauch Chunk Switchback Railroad was abandoned in the 1930s, a short section of track has been rebuilt near the entrance to Mauch Chunk Lake Park. A 1991-built replica of a Switchback car is displayed at the park's entrance. Much of the old right-of-way has been cleared as a bicycle/hiking trail, for which the Switchback Gravity Railroad Foundation publishes a walking tour guide. Brian Solomon

Above: This cast-iron warning sign for the D&H Canal Company was typical of the era. It is displayed at the Reading & Northern offices in Port Clinton, Pennsylvania. Brian Solomon

power to move coal wagons. In *Smoke Stacks and Black Diamonds*, author Joan Campion explains that in preparation for more substantial efforts, a very short demonstration railway was first constructed in the street in Mauch Chunk.

Fulfilling White's vision, Isaac A. Chapman engineered and built a nine-mile gravity tram railway in 1827. Although not the first railroad chartered in Pennsylvania, the Mauch Chunk Gravity Railroad was believed to be the earliest large-scale commercial line constructed in the commonwealth. It was also among the very earliest commercial railways completed in the United States. In *The Kingdom of Coal*, authors Donald L. Miller and Richard E. Sharpless cite researcher and historian Donald Saynga, who wrote that the line used wooden-strap iron rails.

Although its early incarnation had no proper name, the Mauch Chunk Gravity Railroad became known as such because the term "gravity railroad" accurately described how it worked. Once cars were loaded with about one and a half tons of coal, they were hauled by either horses or mules (accounts vary) to the top of a small grade near the mine; from there, gravity forced them downhill to the canal terminal. To keep the progress in check, brakemen rode along with the cars and carefully controlled downhill speed by working a primitive handbrake. At the Mauch Chunk terminal, coal was transferred into waiting boats for shipment downriver. Empty railway cars then were hauled upgrade by mules and returned to the mines for reloading. By some accounts, the horses or mules rode in the cars on the downhill trip.

The success of the railway led to improvements in the mid-1840s. An additional "back track" was laid out parallel to the downhill line. This track incorporated switchbacks and featured inclined planes, which employed stationary steam engines and ropes to hoist cars up steep grades. The arrangement eased the return of empties and largely eliminated the need for animal power, which increased the coal-hauling capacity of the line.

Stereographs such as this one were designed to be viewed with a device known as a stereopticon. This scene, from about 1870, shows the Lehigh Valley Railroad line and adjacent Lehigh Coal & Navigation Company canal in the Lehigh Gorge at Mauch Chunk. Despite the economic superiority of railroads, coal-hauling canals and railroads worked side by side for a number of years. W. A. Lucas, Railroad Museum of Pennsylvania PHMC

The spectacular nature of the gravity railroad and its switchbacks made the site almost an instant tourist attraction. In fact, a special passenger car was built to take visitors over the line, even though the railroad was not originally intended for that purpose. This attraction established an important early link between Pennsylvania's freight-hauling railways and passenger excursions that set a precedent in years to come.

When its usefulness as a coal conveyor ended in about 1872, the Mauch Chunk Gravity Railroad—otherwise known as The Switchback—survived for another six decades as a thrilling downhill train ride for tourists. In fact, the town marketed itself as "The Switzerland of America" because of its rugged mountain scenery, classy hotels, and steep railroads running up the side of the mountain. In the late nineteenth century, Central Railroad of New Jersey looked to augment its coal traffic and capitalize on the growing popularity of the resort town by offering special excursion trains from New York City. More recently, railroad historian Thomas Taber III and others have cited the popular gravity railroad as the predecessor of the amusement park roller coaster.

The line was finally abandoned in 1931, after years of declining ridership and the devastating effects of the Great Depression. While it was the first, and one of the longest surviving gravity lines, it was by no means the only such railway; in fact, it set a pattern for a number of lines that were built in anthracite country.

To move empty coal cars back to the mines at Summit Hill more efficiently, a parallel "back track" was constructed in the 1840s. The track used the steeply inclined Pisgah Plane at Mauch Chunk to lift the cars to the top of the ridge. From there, gravity took its course. In this pre-1873 image of the base of the Pisgah Plane, the Mauch Chunk Switchback Railroad was still moving black diamonds. W. A. Lucas collection, Railroad Museum of Pennsylvania PHMC

Delaware & Hudson and the *Stourbridge Lion*

Many miles north of Mauch Chunk, promoters of the Delaware & Hudson Canal Company embarked upon the most ambitious transportation project of its time—another gravity line—chartered in 1823. The project entailed connecting the mines at Carbondale, Pennsylvania, with markets in New York City. The most challenging part of this scheme was getting coal over the mountains to the canal-head at Honesdale, Pennsylvania. Honesdale was a town named for canal promoter and one-time New York Mayor Philip Hone (1780–1851).

In 1827, D&H's new engineer, John B. Jervis (1795–1885), oversaw a critically important survey between Carbondale and Honesdale. Considering the steep grades and heavy loads that needed to be moved, Jervis designated a route that used five inclined planes on the ascending grade from Carbondale and three inclined planes on the descending grade to Honesdale. (In those days, engineers did not fully understand the principles of adhesion and didn't believe that it was possible for locomotives to work upgrade, so railways were typically laid out as level as possible with grades surmounted by short, steeply graded, rope- or animal-hauled sections known as inclines, or inclined planes.) Jervis also made a pioneering cost analysis of using steam power versus animal haulage, and he compared the costs of using canals versus railroads, concluding in an article reprinted in *A Century of Progress* that "successful accomplishment [of a railroad] will form a new era in the internal improvements to our country." His analysis was especially remarkable considering that in 1827 steam-powered railways did not exist in the United States.

In January 1828, Jervis dispatched engineer Horatio Allen (1802–1899) to Britain to learn about railway practices and to purchase both iron rails and locomotives to import to the United States. Only 26 years old at the time that he was sent to Britain, Allen met with George Stephenson, who is now acknowledged as the father of the railway. Eventually, Allen became one of the foremost railroad experts and proponents of his time.

The first among Allen's British-made locomotives that arrived on U.S. soil was the machine appropriately named *America*, which was built by George Stephenson's son Robert. Not just D&H's first locomotive, this machine also was credited as the first commercially built locomotive to arrive in the United States. Several months later, three locomotives built by Foster, Rastrick & Company of Stourbridge, England, arrived. It was one of these machines, not the *America*, that is normally credited in histories as the first locomotive to operate in the United States. As it turned out, Allen first fired up the *Stourbridge Lion* on August 8, 1829, at Honesdale. He operated it over a distance of three miles and across what was then seen as a perilously tall bridge that carried tracks 30 feet over Lackawaxen Creek. The machine was named for the English village along the River Stour where it was built and was fairly typical of the contraptions used on British colliery lines during

The old Mauch Chunk Switchback Gravity Railroad had two lines, the original down line and the back track. These crossed at a location known as Five Mile Tree, where there was also a connection between the two. This photograph was taken by George M. Hart on October 30, 1937, shortly after the tracks were lifted. They were abandoned in 1931. Today, this location can be reached by hiking the line west from Mauch Chunk Lake Park. W. A. Lucas collection, Railroad Museum of Pennsylvania PHMC

Considering the historical importance of Delaware & Hudson's gravity railroad, very few remnants of the old line have survived. Among the few tangible remains is this stone arch bridge near Keen Lake, Pennsylvania, which is about 10 miles west of Honesdale. Brian Solomon

the Industrial Revolution. It looks peculiar, though, when compared to later locomotives.

Although the *Stourbridge Lion* performed adequately, it was deemed to be too heavy for D&H's lightly built tracks. A second trial with *Stourbridge Lion* a month later proved that operating it would require a substantial and costly upgrade to the D&H railway. Instead of going ahead with that upgrade, the accountants won the day: D&H decided to store its costly imported locomotives rather than invest in improved track. Coal shipment by canal commenced a month

later. In the short term, D&H's coal wagons were hauled by that well-tried method of propulsion: animal power.

Delaware & Hudson profited greatly from coal traffic, which led to expanded operations. Eventually, in addition to its canal, D&H built and operated a network of conventional common carrier steam railroad lines. The railroad eventually reached south to Scranton and Wilkes-Barre and northward into New York State and Canada. D&H's gravity railroad survived for 70 years and outlived its canal by just a few months. The last coal boat navigated the canal on November 5, 1898.

Located along Main Street in Honesdale, Delaware & Hudson Canal Company's modest offices were near the western terminus of its canal, where its gravity railroad delivered coal from mines. Today, the building is the Wayne County Historical Society's museum, and it houses the 1932-built Stourbridge Lion *replica, the D&H gravity car* Eclipse, *as well as various artifacts and photographs relating to the canal and gravity railroad. Although the office has been preserved, not much else remains of the intensive industrial complex that once existed at Honesdale.* Brian Solomon

Credited as the first commercially built reciprocating steam locomotive to operate in the United States, the original Stourbridge Lion *was constructed by Foster, Rastrick & Company in Stourbridge, England. Characteristic of early machines, it used vertical cylinders with rocker arms to transmit power to driving wheels rather than direct connections (typical of most locomotives built after Robert Stephenson's* Rocket *of 1829). This replica was constructed at the D&H's Colonie Shops more than a century after the original was shipped across the Atlantic.* Brian Solomon

The so-called Stourbridge Line *operates seasonally themed passenger excursions over the Honesdale branch of the former Erie Railroad to Hawley. These rides are among the best ways to experience rail transport in the cradle of heavy American railroading. The passenger cars are former Delaware, Lackawanna & Western suburban electric multiple units, while the locomotive is one of the few surviving Electro-Motive model BL2s—a type designed for branch-line work.* Otto M. Vondrak

Visiting Carbondale and Honesdale

Although D&H's Gravity Railroad was once the dominant feature in the historic towns of Carbondale and Honesdale, remarkably little survives of this intensive industrial enterprise. The region has since become a popular tourist destination, but most visitors come for the lakes, mountains, and relative calm of the countryside. They are largely oblivious to the history of the gravity railroad and canals.

At Honesdale, where D&H's gravity railroad met the canal head, modern visitors can enjoy several interesting sites. On Main Street, near the corner of Eighth Street and adjacent to the Honesdale Post Office, is the dignified brick and brownstone building that once served as headquarters for the D&H Canal Company.

Now a museum operated by the Wayne County Historical Society, it houses a collection of photographs, maps, artifacts, and equipment relating to the D&H Canal Company. Inside, visitors are treated to an authentic reproduction of the *Stourbridge Lion*, built in 1932 at D&H's Colonie Shops near Watervliet, New York. It is decorated with a stylized lion's head.

Among the displays is an item that relates the mysterious tale of the *America*. Was this locomotive simply stored and never used, as many historians have reported, or rather was it really the first commercial locomotive tested in the United States and then met an unfortunate end? Also on display is the *Eclipse*, an actual D&H passenger car used on the gravity railroad. Built in 1882, this 29-foot-3-inch-long passenger carriage shows how small D&H's gravity passenger cars really were on the line. With just 20 seats, the *Eclipse* is claustrophobic when compared with standard-size passenger cars. One of the few surviving relics of D&H's gravity railroad, this car is also unusual because it is a luxury coach.

Additional exhibits include a model of a canal lock, authentic tools used to build canal boats including a wooden foot-operated lathe, and lumps of the actual anthracite that played such an important role in the area's history.

Behind the museum are the tracks of the Lackawaxen & Stourbridge, a short-line railroad that operates the old Honesdale branch. *The Stourbridge Line*, with an Electro-Motive BL2 diesel-electric and vintage passenger cars, runs excursions along the route. Seasonal trips travel the length of the Erie's Honesdale branch to Hawley, about 10 miles to the east. Hawley was once the terminus of the Pennsylvania Coal Company's gravity line, similar to D&H's pioneering operation. Later, Hawley was the junction between the branch and Erie's coal-hauling Erie Railroad Wyoming division main line between Lackawaxen and Scranton, which replaced the aforementioned gravity railroad in the 1880s. The Erie's line over the mountain to the west was abandoned in the 1960s, but its tracks are still in place to Lackawaxen, where they connect with the old Erie Delaware division. As of 2007, that line was operated as a subsidiary of the New York, Susquehanna & Western. Yet, a damaged bridge on the Erie branch east of Hawley has precluded regular excursions to Lackawaxen in recent years.

In its day, the Delaware & Hudson Gravity Railroad was a dominant feature in the village of Honesdale. This view, near the head of the canal basin, shows one of the inclined planes. Although the railroad was primarily used in the conveyance of coal, it also carried passengers. Part of this plane is now a city street. W. A. Lucas collection, Railroad Museum of Pennsylvania PHMC

Stourbridge Line passenger cars are typically stored on the sidings to the south of Main Street in Honesdale. Three are former Delaware, Lackawanna & Western electric suburban cars that carry the names of those famous for their involvement with the D&H: car No. 3509 is *Irad Hawley*, for whom Hawleyville is named; car No. 3519 is the *John Roebling*, the legendary bridge engineer who designed several of the canal aqueducts; and car No. 3596 is the *Philip Hone*. Another car, a classic heavyweight all-steel one, is named *Horatio Allen*.

Just south of the L&S tracks, and along a street that was once parallel to the right-of-way occupied by D&H's gravity railroad, is the Wayne County Chamber of Commerce. Outside the building is a replica of a gravity coal car, complete with a load of real anthracite. Inside is a model of the old gravity line.

Among the few vestiges of the gravity railroad are portions of stone arch bridges located in a campground off Highway 6, about 10 miles west of Honesdale on the north shore of Keen Lake.

CHAPTER 2

HISTORICAL ANTHRACITE RAILROADS

The demand for coal and success of the early gravity railroads spurred Pennsylvania's first railroad mania. By the end of the 1820s, dozens of lines were under consideration. During the first half of the 1830s, railroad construction in the state largely focused on the anthracite region. Visions of the grand profits encouraged railroad competitors to build many systems of railway lines in this area.

At first, these railways were designed to feed and augment the canal network. Yet, as the railways became more efficient, their owners pushed to carry a larger share of traffic. Eventually, the anthracite railways duplicated and superseded the canals and took over more and more territory and traffic. This competition produced one of most intensely developed and overlapping railroad networks in the United States; valleys were thick with track, as two or more companies reached to tap the flow of anthracite. As the network developed, trains hauled a greater variety of commodities, and the railroads developed passenger services.

Prior to the Civil War, the anthracite boom fueled the growth of an iron industry in eastern Pennsylvania that produced America's first intensive industrial revolution. Boomtowns such as Scranton, Reading, Bethlehem, and Allentown rapidly grew around coal and iron mines, furnaces, foundries, and related industries. The perfection of the steam locomotive was crucial to this rapid railroad expansion. In Britain, Robert Stephenson's *Rocket* of 1829 had successfully combined three crucial

Facing page: The Conrail years were not kind to former anthracite routes. When Conrail assumed operation in 1976, the once-busy lines had suffered from decades of neglect and relatively light traffic. Conrail focused on making the "Blue Giant" profitable and spared no tears for under-utilized routes. It hacked away many miles of former Lehigh Valley, Reading Company, and Lackawanna lines from the map. In October 1991, a westward Conrail ALCG (a symbol freight that worked between Allentown and Gang Mills Yard near Corning, New York) led by SD40-2 6414 roars up through the Lehigh Gorge on the former LVRR. The old, westward main track was then derelict, but it has since been restored to service by Reading & Northern. The parallel right-of-way of the old Central Railroad of New Jersey line had been abandoned prior to Conrail, but it has since been converted into a rail-trail. Scott R. Snell

Above: Lehigh & New England was a bridge railroad that connected eastern Pennsylvania with Campbell Hall, New York. From there, freight traffic traveled to New England via the New Haven Railroad. L&NE once thrived on anthracite and cement traffic. Although most of the railroad was liquidated in 1961, several of its freight cars and a caboose survive on the Wanamaker, Kempton & Southern. One branch of the old L&NE operated on the north side of Blue Mountain, just a few miles north of the old Reading Company branch now operated by the W&KS. The L&NE logo reflects that of the Lehigh Coal & Navigation Company, which owned the line. Brian Solomon

This glass plate view of Easton, Pennsylvania, dates from the late-nineteenth century. Looking north-northeast, it shows the tracks of Lehigh Valley Railroad in the foreground and those of Central Railroad of New Jersey lines beyond, including the railroad's 1892 through and deck truss bridges over the Lehigh River and Lehigh Canal. The two lines ran parallel into anthracite country and competed directly for traffic. Today, the Lehigh Line remains an important Norfolk Southern freight route through Easton. Railroad Museum of Pennsylvania PHMC

concepts: a multitubular (fire tube) boiler, forced draft from exhaust steam, and direct linkage between the piston and drive wheels. When in operation, the forced draft caused the fire to burn hotter and the boiler to generate steam more quickly, which allowed the locomotive to produce greater power as it operated faster.

The *Rocket* set the pattern for all subsequent reciprocating steam locomotive designs. It provides an excellent analogy in the "multiplier effect" for the railroad's role in the industrial revolution: As the primary conduit for both iron and coal, successful railroads made production and delivery of commercial iron cheaper than ever before, while the railroad itself was the primary consumer of both commodities. The locomotive was the iron horse and rode on an iron road, so as the railroad expanded and increased capacity, its demands drove the plants it served. The anthracite and iron boom in eastern Pennsylvania set the pattern for the even more intensive industrial expansion, focused on bituminous coal and

steel production, around which Pittsburgh flourished in the late nineteenth century.

Philadelphia & Reading

Incorporated to connect its namesake cities on April 4, 1833, Philadelphia & Reading suffered from inadequate funds, which impaired its early construction. The line was engineered by one of the early masters of railroad building—Moncure Robinson (1802–1891). Robinson had previously engineered the Allegheny Portage Railroad (see Part III) and initially planned for the Reading line to be an anthracite hauler. Yet, according to the Reading Company's Jay V. Hare's serialized history of the company, the railroad subsisted on passenger revenue until its line was ready to haul freight.

Philadelphia & Reading's first passenger service began on May 1, 1838, between Reading and Pottstown. The fare was 75 cents, which was deemed a considerable sum. P&R's line opened from Reading to

Philadelphia in December 1839, and its first through train carried 240 tons of freight and 60 passengers. This train, with a maximum speed of only 12 miles per hour, took nine hours to reach Philadelphia. Its glacial speed was attributed to the failure of P&R's new locomotive, *Gowan & Marx*, which was one of the first 4-4-0 American types. The American type went on to become the most popular wheel arrangement of the nineteenth century, and it was used on thousands of railroads across the country.

P&R rose to dominate the southern anthracite fields. It built, bought, leased, and controlled various lines. Its coal routes blanketed the region spanning the lower Delaware River Valley to the Susquehanna River and reached north from Philadelphia toward Allentown and Bethlehem, and northwest from Reading to dozens of coal-producing towns, including Pottsville, Mahanoy City, Tamaqua, and Shamokin. As the railroad prospered, it reached beyond the anthracite fields to secure connections and expand its markets. Lines ran southwest of Reading via Harrisburg to Lurgan and Gettysburg to interchange with the Western Maryland; northwest to Newberry Junction near Williamsport to interchange with the Fall Brook Route—later New York Central; and northeast across New Jersey to its

The steam whistle is among the icons of the era. The tone and pitch of whistles are varied. Some locomotives have a low, mournful wail that stirs the soul when sounded across a river valley. Other locomotive whistles are more shrill and designed to catch the immediate attention of trespassers or motorists at grade crossings. Middletown & Hummelstown No. 91 sounds off before departing the Middletown yard. Brian Solomon

In the 1960s, Reading Company operated passenger excursions with its home-built Class T-1 4-8-4 steam locomotives. Its Reading Rambles covered various anthracite lines in eastern Pennsylvania. Several of Reading's T-1s have been preserved, including No. 2124, which is now displayed at Steamtown in Scranton. Likewise, a number of historic railways acquired Reading Company steel passenger cars such as those pictured here in October 1963. Richard Jay Solomon

own Atlantic access port, appropriately named Port Reading on the Arthur Kill near Perth Amboy.

Not only was P&R master of its territory, but in the second half of the nineteenth century, the company aimed to dominate the whole anthracite industry. At its peak, it controlled the Central Railroad of New Jersey

This former Reading Company caboose was typical of eight-wheel cabooses used on freight trains all over Pennsylvania. In addition to serving as an office and bunk car, the caboose was a marker at the rear of a freight train. The color of lamps displayed at the back had specific meanings, depending on the direction and class of the train. Before a train could be considered "complete" within the operating rules, it was necessary to display appropriate flags or lamps at the back. This caboose is preserved in service on the Wanamaker, Kempton & Southern.
Brian Solomon

and Lehigh Valley, with ambitious schemes that led to its financial insolvency on more than one occasion. P&R's independence ended after one such financial collapse and, in 1893, legendary financier J. P. Morgan assumed control of the company. From then on, P&R was known as the Reading Company. In the twentieth century, as it remained the foremost hauler of anthracite, its operation and finances were closely tied to the Baltimore & Ohio, which controlled it. B&O used Reading's and CNJ's lines to reach the New York metro area.

Lehigh Valley Railroad

The Lehigh Valley Railroad began as the Delaware, Lehigh, Schuylkill & Susquehanna, chartered in April 1846. While its name was a mouthful encompassing every major river in the region except the Hudson, the railroad aimed to provide competition to a transportation monopoly held by Lehigh Coal & Navigation Company canals in the Lehigh Valley.

As with other early lines, this railroad developed slowly in its formative years. It wasn't until coal magnate Asa Packer (1805–1879) took control of the line in 1851 that the railroad really got going. Under Packer's leadership, the railroad not only changed its name, but it built east along the Lehigh River to connect Mauch Chunk with Easton by 1855. At Easton, LV reached the Delaware Canal, the recently extended Central Railroad of New Jersey, and the Bel-Del line of the PRR. A later extension pushed the LV through the Lehigh Gorge to White Haven.

Gradually, Packer and his chief engineer Robert H. Sayre (1824–1907) expanded the network to build branch lines through mergers. Lehigh Valley tapped farther into Wyoming Valley coal fields with acquisition of the well-established Beaver Meadows Railroad in 1864, the Lehigh & Mahanoy in 1865, and Hazelton Railroad in 1868. Lehigh Valley pushed its main line over Penobscot Mountain—which divides the Lehigh Valley from the valley of the north branch of the Susquehanna—and reached northwest to the New York state line, where it connected with the Erie Railroad. Later, as CNJ, its one-time eastward connection, expanded west into anthracite country, Lehigh Valley extended its path eastward. By 1889, the railroad reached the Hudson River at Jersey City, opposite Manhattan. Not only did Lehigh Valley continue to extend branches in the Wyoming Valley, often overlapping

An 1883 view looks east across Delaware to the Lackawanna & Western's yards and shops at Scranton. Today, this site is occupied by Steamtown. In the foreground, note DL&W's line to Northumberland that served as its primary anthracite feeder. Just beyond it is Bridge 60 over the Lackawanna River, which was then a stone arch, but in 1907 it was replaced by the present plate girder structure. Freight yards are at the center left and various shop buildings are at the right. Thomas T. Taber collection, Railroad Museum of Pennsylvania PHMC

This period photo shows Delaware, Lackawanna & Western 4-4-0 Class G-5 camelback No. 952 at the Scranton shops. It was once a standard type on the railroad, but No. 952 is now one of only two surviving examples of DL&W steam power. It is also one of only a handful of surviving camelbacks. The locomotive was saved from scrapping in 1939, and since 1953 it has been displayed at the National Museum of Transport in Kirkwood, Missouri. Thomas T. Taber collection, Railroad Museum of Pennsylvania PHMC

with P&R's lines, but it completed its own route to Buffalo, New York, in 1892. This crucial gateway formed a link for a through route to the Midwest and Canada for the movement of coal, merchandise freight, and passenger traffic.

Delaware, Lackawanna & Western

Another railroad—long synonymous with hard coal and known as The Road of Anthracite—was the Delaware, Lackawanna & Western. The Lackawanna was famous for its early twentieth-century advertising featuring the pure, demure, and fictional passenger Phoebe Snow.

The road began in Scranton in 1849 as a broad gauge feeder to the Erie Railroad and was known as the DL&W after 1853. Initially running just from Scranton to the Erie at Great Bend, it later extended a line eastward

across the Poconos to the Delaware River near Stroudsburg. Like the Lehigh Valley, this railroad gradually built east and west to connect the west shore of the Hudson opposite New York City (at Hoboken) with Buffalo, New York. It also built secondary lines to Utica; to the coal port on Lake Ontario at Oswego, New York; as well as established branches in Pennsylvania's coal country. Earning a healthy profit from anthracite haulage, DL&W operations were focused at Scranton, where it built yards and shops.

When William H. Truesdale assumed control of the line in 1899, he transformed DL&W into a super railroad through skillful management and massive capital improvements to the company's essential infrastructure. He built modern passenger and freight terminals, upgraded the road's New York area facilities with the

TRESTLE OVER LACKAWANNA RIVER AND ARCH UNDER CONSTRUCTION
View looking West from Lackawanna Avenue and Cliff Street

This multiple-tier wooden trestle was DL&W's original crossing of the Lackawanna River at Scranton. It is seen on September 4, 1866, shortly before it was replaced with a stone arch. The stone arch bridge was subsequently replaced with the present plate girder structure known as Bridge 60, and it is used today by Steamtown excursions and Delaware-Lackawanna freights. At the time of this photograph, DL&W still used broad gauge tracks and interchanged with the Erie. Thomas T. Taber collection Railroad Museum of Pennsylvania PHMC

state-of-the-art Hoboken Terminal, and constructed new shops and yards in Scranton. Truesdale's engineers reprofiled Lackawanna's mountain main lines by relocating alignments to lower maximum gradients, reducing curvature, shortening routes, and reducing both operating and maintenance expenses. The famed Lackawanna Cutoff in western New Jersey, built in 1908, shortened the railroad's Hoboken-to-Buffalo route. Then in 1915, the railroad built the Summit Cutoff that reduced grades on the line over Clarks Summit between Scranton and Binghamton and included the famous Tunkhannock and Martins Creek viaducts. With its improved line, Lackawanna hoped to redefine its role and gain greater amounts of bridge traffic to augment its anthracite business.

Central Railroad of New Jersey

By spanning its namesake state by 1853, Central Railroad of New Jersey developed a bridge route for anthracite moving via Lehigh Valley and Delaware, Lackawanna & Western traffic to the New York metro area and beyond. Author Elaine Anderson explains in *The Central Railroad of New Jersey's First 100 Years* that while CNJ was built to standard gauge (4 feet, 8.5 inches) in order to accommodate DL&W's six-foot gauge cars, CNJ built some its line with dual gauge track—a very unusual arrangement in America railroading.

By the early 1870s, Lehigh Valley and DL&W had extended their empires east of the Delaware River, which encouraged CNJ to push west into anthracite country. In April 1871, it leased the recently completed Lehigh & Susquehanna from the Lehigh Coal & Navigation Company and took its line to White Haven via Mauch Chunk. From there, CNJ eventually reached Scranton. Much of its route was parallel to Lehigh Valley, and in many places the two railroads ran side by side. After the Civil War, changes in the law made railroad acquisition of coal land and mines easier, thus allowing railroads to invest more heavily in the business of mining and transporting coal. Like the other railroads in the region, CNJ acquired coal resources, although its holdings were much less than P&R's extensive anthracite properties.

Trunk Lines in Anthracite Country

Anthracite traffic attracted the east-west trunk lines, too. In *Centennial History of the Pennsylvania Railroad*, authors George H. Burgess and Miles C. Kennedy note

that while PRR didn't reach the anthracite fields directly in the 1860s, it tapped this traffic through its Northern Central, Philadelphia & Erie, and Pennsylvania Canal Company affiliates. After the Civil War, P&R and other railroads began a frantic land grab for coal-rich property. PRR moved to secure for itself a place in anthracite country by acquiring more than 28,000 acres, mostly along tributaries of the Susquehanna. In the 1880s, when PRR vied for territory with the

The former Central Railroad of New Jersey freight house along Lackawanna Avenue in Scranton is evidence of that railroad's presence in the city. At its peak, CNJ was a significant anthracite hauler; it connected Scranton and Wilkes-Barre with markets in New York City. After 1910, CNJ's passenger trains to Scranton used DL&W's magnificent new station located several blocks farther east of this building on Lackawanna Avenue. In Scranton, CNJ followed the west bank of the Lackawanna River—opposite the Delaware & Hudson line— and portions now serve as a hiking trail. Brian Solomon

Reading and New York Central, it pushed a line northward from Philadelphia along the Schuylkill River into the anthracite fields that closely paralleled P&R's.

The Erie Railroad penetrated anthracite country by building and acquiring lines in the Wyoming Valley. Erie's Wyoming division extended west from its main line at Lackawaxen—the location of John Roebling's famous canal bridge over the Delaware—to Dunmore and Pittston. Its Jefferson division cut south from a junction at the west end of the Starrucca Viaduct near Lanesboro and went over Ararat Summit to Carbondale and Scranton. As built, this line was shared with Delaware & Hudson, which used it to reach its own main line to Albany, New York, and beyond.

Competition

Although fiercely competitive, anthracite railroads were incestuous companies and cooperated when it suited them. In the late nineteenth century, Philadelphia & Reading's officers had dreams of a virtual anthracite monopoly. By that time, its lines blanketed some 75 percent of the mining region, making it by far the largest conveyor of anthracite coal. In 1883, Reading took control of Central Railroad of New Jersey, only to lose it again following financial distress. Still, CNJ and Reading remained closely coordinated. Their systems fit together neatly, as CNJ tapped northern fields and fed traffic east to New York and New England, while Reading tapped southern fields and moved coal to Philadelphia. Together, they provided a through route between Philadelphia and the New York metro area, as well as through routes between New York and Harrisburg and Williamsport—all important coal gateways.

Other railroads fought for similar traffic, and in many places duplicative lines were built. While parallel sets of tracks might seem unnecessary and wasteful

Philadelphia & Reading (after 1893, the Reading Company) amassed a fortune mining and hauling anthracite, but from its earliest days it also developed a significant passenger business. Prior to World War I, it invested in a fleet of all-steel coaches built by The Harlan & Hollingsworth Corporation. Today, some of these cars are still used by the Wanamaker, Kempton & Southern, which operates steam- and diesel-hauled excursions on a rustic former Reading Company branch line. Brian Solomon

THE BLACK DIAMOND

Call it stone coal, black diamonds, or anthracite, the original impetus and driving force behind the railroads in the region was the movement of coal. Its importance was clearly manifested in company heralds, train names, and advertising. Reading, Lehigh Valley, and Erie were among lines that used the diamond herald—emblematic of "black diamonds." Lehigh Valley's most famous train, the *Black Diamond* conveyed the spirit of the railroad that could boast it was literally and figuratively the "Route of the Black Diamond."

Named passenger trains were a railroad's most important public relations and advertising tool. With its passenger service, a railroad promoted its route, demonstrated its loyalty to the region it served, and inspired shippers to use its lines for freight. In this, the *Black Diamond* was among the best. It also was known for its high levels of comfort and speed records—albeit on the relatively level tangent track near Buffalo, not in the twisting confines of the Lehigh Gorge. By 1906, the *Black Diamond Limited* had an international reputation. In the 1930s, Lehigh Valley followed a national trend by streamlining the train. The company hauled it with dressed up Pacifics adorned in futuristic shrouds designed by Otto Kuhler.

The consist for Lehigh Valley's Black Diamond *posed westbound at Easton on May 14, 1896—four days prior to its inaugural run. Leading is a 4-4-0 American-type locomotive designed for fast passenger service. It also features the camelback arrangement with a wide firebox for burning anthracite culm. Note the passenger cars, the best from Pullman— finely varnished, heavy wooden 12-wheelers designed for a comfortable ride. The* Black Diamond *would soon become one of the most famous trains in the world.* Thomas T. Taber collection, Railroad Museum of Pennsylvania PHMC

Working east from Scranton, Delaware–Lackawanna's PT98 is heading upgrade along Roaring Brook toward Pocono Summit on the old DL&W main line. The old Lackawanna shared Roaring Brook Valley with Erie Railroad's Wyoming division, which ran eastward. One of Erie's derelict bridges can be seen here to the left of the DL freight. The breakup of Conrail in 1999 resulted in the restoration of the old DL&W main line via Pocono Summit as a through route to Slateford Junction. Patrick Yough

today, they weren't so at the time. The growing tide of anthracite was flooding region's railways, which were also handling a fair amount of merchandise business and passenger travel. Not only were parallel main lines necessary to keep trains moving, but as traffic increased, railroads added main tracks with sections of directional double track, sections of triple track, and even quadruple main-line track.

One of the most complex track arrangements was in the Scranton/Wilkes-Barre region, where at one time no less than eight Class 1 railroad carriers vied for traffic in surrounding valleys. Except for the Reading, which never reached the region, the lines already mentioned served this area, plus late-comers New York, Ontario & Western, and New York Susquehanna & Western's Pennsylvania affiliate Wilkes-Barre & Eastern. There were also two third-rail electric interurban lines and city streetcar companies.

Decline and Fall of Anthracite Empires

Seeing the multitude of abandoned lines and underutilized track that remain from these historic anthracite

Lehigh Valley's Budd-built rail diesel car No. 40 makes a connection with a through train at Lehighton for Hazelton on March 27, 1959. The Philadelphia-based Budd Company was a significant innovator and producer of streamlined passenger equipment and developed the self-propelled RDC as an economical solution for branch-line and commuter train operations. Today, old LV No. 40 is preserved at the Railroad Museum of Pennsylvania at Strasburg. Richard Jay Solomon

railroads begs the question of what ever happened to this vast network. Anthracite railroads were so closely tied to the mineral that had coaxed them into the lush valleys that when this traffic dried up, so did the railways that tapped it. The region once saturated with railways eventually saw numerous line abandonments.

On a national level, the greed, mismanagement, and compulsive overbuilding by railroads in the nineteenth century sparked financial tremors that seemed to threaten the very economic fabric of the nation. Rate pools, gross misuse of the public trust, and callous actions by the railroad's top management resulted in public backlash. Gradually, Congress enacted legislation to even the score. The Sherman Anti-Trust Act and Hepburn Act forced a separation of anthracite railroads from their coal property.

After World War I, the demand for anthracite waned as bituminous coal, and later oil and natural gas, developed as a popular home heating and industrial fuel. Even the anthracite railroads moved away from steam locomotives designed to burn hard coal. The change did take several years, and demand for anthracite remained robust into the 1920s. In *The Central Railroad of New Jersey's First 100 Years*, author Elaine Anderson writes that in 1926 CNJ alone moved 1,154,333 cars of coal, much of it anthracite, yet the writing was on the wall. Bitter strikes had caused work stoppages in the anthracite mines. The resulting fuel shortages encouraged home owners to abandon hard coal. Once they switched, they never switched back.

Then the Great Depression hit the anthracite business hard. The first significant carrier to vacate the

March 27, 1959, was a dull spring day when this Lehigh Valley train paused for its station stop in Jim Thorpe. Never a major passenger carrier, Lehigh Valley saw its passenger miles drop 90 percent between World War II and 1960. By 1961, it abandoned all passenger services, which put it among the first important railroads in the East to become an entirely freight-only line. Richard Jay Solomon

region was Wilkes-Barre & Eastern, which abandoned its lines in 1939. To survive, other anthracite railroads looked increasingly to other industries to keep their lines busy and sustain their bottom lines. However, with increased regulations and a decline in anthracite use, there came another hard blow: growing emphasis on public roads. As roads improved, trucks siphoned away merchandise business, and the use of private cars eroded railroad passenger traffic. World War II thrust traffic back to the rails for a few years, but by the mid-1950s, anthracite country was laced with parallel and often redundant lines.

Some carriers considered consolidation. Others—like New York, Ontario & Western, a railroad that through the late 1930s had enjoyed robust coal traffic on its Scranton division but had been in bankruptcy for decades—gave up. O&W was completely liquidated in March 1957 with its service suspended, tracks lifted,

and equipment sold at auction. In 1960, Erie Railroad and Delaware, Lackawanna & Western, which had operated parallel systems between Jersey City and Buffalo, merged to form Erie Lackawanna with the hope that eliminating redundant lines and combining routes would allow it to survive. A few years later, CNJ and Lehigh Valley consolidated their grossly underutilized lines in Pennsylvania, although they maintained corporate independence from one another. (CNJ under Reading control was in the B&O camp, while Lehigh Valley was controlled by the PRR.) By this time, the great passenger trains in the region were gone; Lehigh Valley had been freight only since 1961.

Already on tenuous ground as the 1970s dawned, railroad finances in the Northeast reached grim new lows. When CNJ, which had only emerged from bankruptcy in 1949, declared bankruptcy again in 1969, it was a whisper of doom for the brewing storm to come. PRR and its arch competitor New York Central had merged in 1968 to form Penn Central. The hopes that consolidation-related efficiencies would curb their financial woes soon proved futile. PC's problems were complex; it suffered from operating inefficiencies, ineffective government rate regulation, antiquated labor agreements, decaying facilities, heavy passenger deficits, and poor state tax policies, as well as intense highway competition. All of this was compounded by PC mismanagement and corporate infighting. When Penn Central declared bankruptcy in 1970, it sent a shock through the railroad industry and government. By this time, the old anthracite roads that were once some of the richest and busiest properties had become fragile fossils that were waiting for the grave. In the wake of the PC collapse, they, too, descended into bankruptcy.

Conrail

When eastern railroading collapsed into a financial maelstrom, it forced the federal government to take action. The result was the Conrail bailout of 1976. From April 1 of that year, northeastern roads Penn Central, Erie Lackawanna, Lehigh Valley, Central Railroad of New Jersey, Reading Co., and Lehigh & Hudson came under the Conrail banner. After absorbing billions of federal dollars, and being helped by the deregulation mandated by the Staggers Act of 1980, Conrail finally was profitable under the Stanley Crane administration in the 1980s.

Part of Conrail's mandate was to trim redundant lines. So, it gradually trimmed its network. Many of the lines that were part of Conrail in 1976 were abandoned, sold, or closed in the 1970s and 1980s. As Conrail shed trackage, other railroads picked up the pieces. A host of new short lines and regional lines soon ran on these rails, which also paved the way for a new era of railway preservation and excursion train operation.

Built in 1881, the former Lehigh Valley passenger station at Sayre, Pennsylvania, sat opposite the railroad's shops along the railroad's main line. In its heyday, Sayre was a busy railroad shop town, with a division headquarters and large freight yards, and it was the place where crew changes were made. The importance of Sayre was greatly diminished with the decline of Lehigh Valley; its fate was sealed when LV became part of Conrail in 1976. Today, the station is restored, and it is home to the Sayre Historical Society Museum. Brian Solomon

Conrail tended to favor keeping former PC routes and facilities. Many of the old anthracite lines were reduced to dead-end branches, and their yards and facilities were consolidated. Redundant lines were abandoned and lifted or left derelict. One exception was east of Harrisburg where the old PRR main line became part

Old coal breakers, such as the derelict St. Nicholas Breaker seen here, dot the landscape in eastern Pennsylvania as a reminder of the anthracite legacy for which the region is famous. Scott R. Snell

Anthracite flowed over the DL&W to myriad points across its system and all over the East. While much of the railroad is now gone, remnants of its coal empire are still evident. Although the tracks to it are long gone, this old coal elevator at South Waverly, near Sayre, still bears an advertisement for DL&W coal. The old Lackawanna main line ran roughly parallel to the Erie's between Binghamton and Corning, New York, and in a few places it skirted the border with Pennsylvania. Here, the tracks were on the Pennsylvania side of the line, although Erie's were in New York State. Brian Solomon

Reading & Northern operates a network of former Reading Company, Lehigh Valley, Central Railroad of New Jersey, and Pennsylvania Railroad lines in anthracite country north and west of Reading, Pennsylvania. This R&N freight passes the restored former Reading Company station at Tamaqua. The oldest portions of the station date to 1874 and served scheduled passenger trains for 99 years. Patrick Yough

of Amtrak's system. To avoid Amtrak charges for routing freight over former PRR electrified routes, Conrail shifted the bulk of its traffic to Philadelphia and New York in the 1980s to use routes consisting of former Reading, Lehigh Valley, and CNJ lines. In 1981, Conrail retired its fleet of former PRR electrics. Over the next decades, it scaled back operation of PRR's heavily constructed freight lines east of Harrisburg. Even PRR's massive Enola Yards (across the Susquehanna from Harrisburg)—once the largest facility of its kind—saw reduced activity. By contrast, some of the anthracite lines' facilities, such as the old CNJ yard at Allentown, were developed as important regional hubs.

Because of skillful management and deregulation, eastern railroading saw a freight renaissance in the 1990s. Still, the nature of railroading had changed.

Most freight now moved in long, intermodal trains carrying highway trailers and containers from regional hubs over long distances. Some carload trains remained, but by this time anthracite traffic, once the lifeblood of lines in eastern Pennsylvania, represented only a fraction of what it once was. Bituminous coal in western Pennsylvania, still an importance source of traffic, moved as unit trains from mine to power plant or waterfront docks for export.

Conrail's success led it to be sold in a public stock offering in 1986. In 1996, CSX and Norfolk Southern entered a bidding war for control of the line, which saw the two lines divide Conrail's former tracks between their huge eastern systems. Most of Conrail's remaining anthracite region trackage was conveyed to NS.

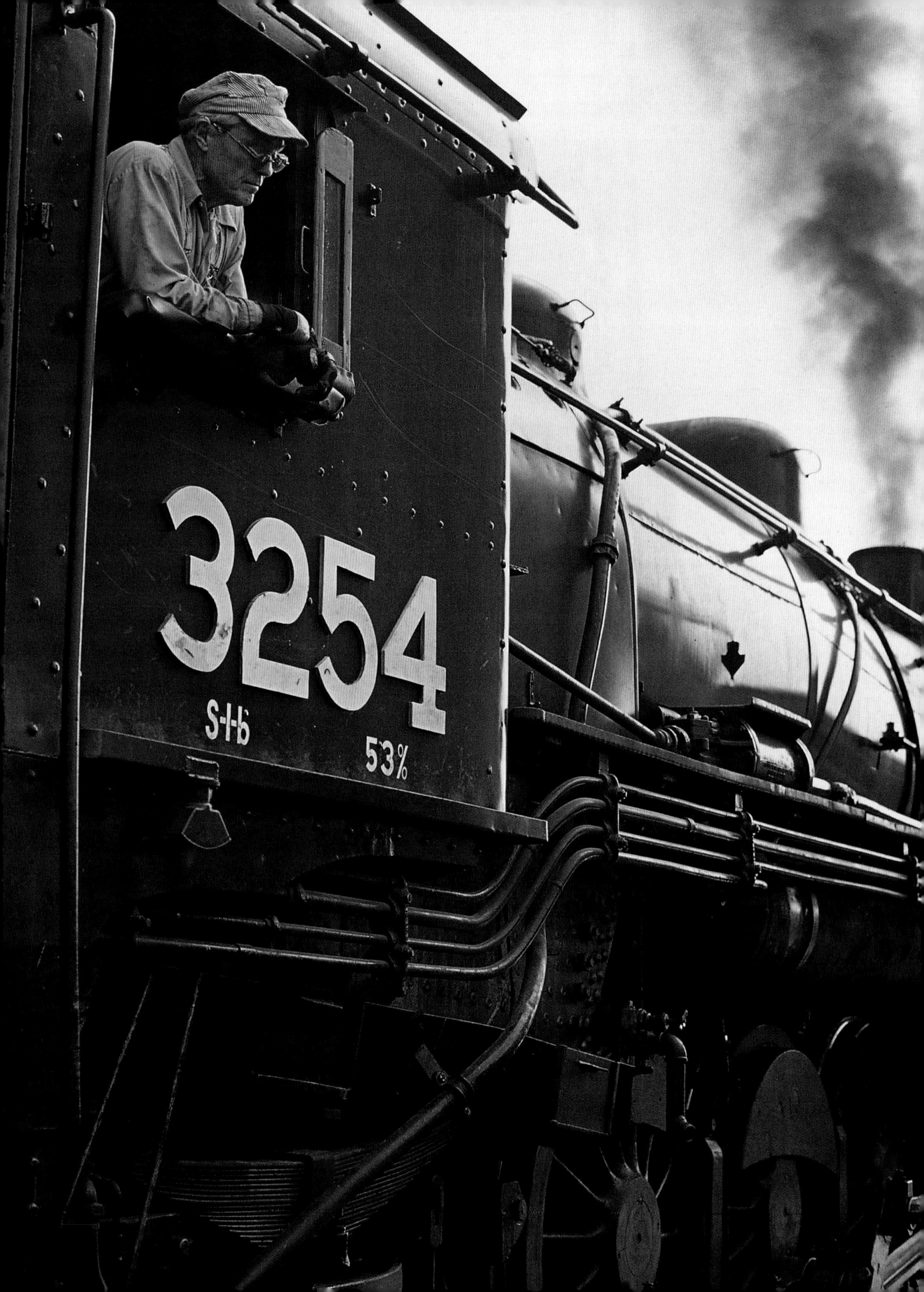
3254
S-1-b
53%

CHAPTER 3

STEAMTOWN

The present-day railroad museum at Steamtown in Scranton is among the most significant railroad sites in Pennsylvania. Situated in the heart of an urban industrial environment, Steamtown provides a great environment to learn about railroading, observe historic equipment, and experience a steam-era shop complex, as well as take a train ride. Steamtown's various facets, complex history, and unique environment make it a fascinating place to visit and experience railroading.

Steamtown's facilities are the heart of the old Delaware, Lackawanna & Western, but its equipment comes from a variety of railroads in the United States and Canada. Although the U.S. National Park Service, which operates Steamtown, has made efforts to acquire DL&W railroad cars and locomotives, Steamtown is not a DL&W museum. Patrick McKnight, Steamtown's resident historian, explains that Steamtown is a blend of its three major components: the old Steamtown Foundation Collection, Scranton's DL&W site, and the National Park Service.

Steamtown began as a private collection of steam locomotives and vintage rairoad cars assembled by the late Nelson Blount at the end of the American steam era. By the time Blount began collecting equipment in the late 1950s, most American railroads were fully dieselized. In addition, a great deal of the more historically significant steam locomotives had already been scrapped. Blount collected locomotives from a variety of lines, including a good selection of modern Canadian steam. Tragically, Blount died in a plane crash in 1966. At that time, his Steamtown collection was in Riverside, near Bellows Falls, Vermont. Seasonal excursions using the steam trains ran over the Green Mountain Railroad until autumn of 1983. Under the direction of the late Don Ball Jr., Steamtown relocated in 1986 to the DL&W site in Scranton, which the state of Pennsylvania acquired from Conrail specifically for that purpose.

DL&W's Scranton shops were first constructed in 1855. Over the years, the railroad adapted and expanded them, with some of the most significant

Facing page: Steamtown recreates the aura and atmosphere of big-time steam railroading. Sitting high in his Mikado, this engineer waits for the signal from the conductor. Only then will he set this magnificent machine into motion for the pleasure of onlookers. Once a common sight in towns across America, big steam locomotives are only maintained and operated in a few places today. Brian Solomon

Above: Displayed in Scranton yard are three Delaware, Lackawanna & Western anthracite coal hoppers. Once common, anthracite movements through Scranton are as rare today. The preservation of freight equipment that operated in the same period as the locomotives preserved at Steamtown has been among the goals of the park service. Brian Solomon

improvements coming under the William Truesdale administration beginning in 1895. As the new freight facilities—including Taylor Yard, built southwest of downtown—assumed much of the work once handled by DL&W's downtown yards, the yards transformed to accommodate local traffic.

After World War II, DL&W, like most American railroads, aggressively phased out steam operations and replaced them with diesels. Because diesels needed less heavy maintenance than steam locomotives, DL&W scaled back the scope of its facilities. After closing its old erecting shops at the east end of the facility, the U.S. Army occupied them in 1951. The army has since used them as a heavy machine shop for constructing shell casings. With Erie Lackawanna and Conrail's Scranton's role diminished by the early 1980s, the shops and downtown yards were largely derelict, sad reminders of better days.

After the Steamtown National Historic Site was created on October 30, 1986, and the National Park Service took over its management, the park service made a concerted effort to acquire significant pieces of rolling stock for display in Scranton. Over the last 20 years, a number of former DL&W cars and locomotives, as well as those from other anthracite railroads, have been added to the collection. Other equipment, deemed inappropriate for the site, has moved to better homes.

As a result of the National Park Service's efforts, Steamtown's visitor's center and museum emulates the spirit of a classic railroad roundhouse environment. Here, the park service has blended surviving portions of the old DL&W roundhouse with new buildings that echo the design of early twentieth-century railroad structures. Situated around the turntable, authentically restored locomotives and freight cars are posed to illustrate the types of equipment used by the region's railroads in the middle of the twentieth century.

Inside, the buildings have interpretive exhibits that explain various aspects of North American railroading and offer a crash course in classic railroad history. Among the displays, various railroad jobs—station master, conductor, locomotive engineer, brakemen, and switchmen—are profiled. Taped video documentaries of railroaders convey their experiences. The exhibits also highlight some of the less pleasant

Steamtown keeps the spirit of heavy steam railroading alive at the former DL&W shops and roundhouse in Scranton. The roundhouse was built in 1902, partly destroyed by fire in 1917, and expanded again in 1937. Steamtown's demonstration trains are operated using steam and vintage diesel-electric locomotives along with World War I vintage steel heavyweight passenger cars. A regular on these trains is the Canadian National Railway's Mikado-type steam locomotive No. 3254. The Mikado is defined by its 2-8-2 wheel arrangement and was the most common type of steam locomotive used in North America in the twentieth century. Brian Solomon

This view from the cab of a Delaware-Lackawanna Alco Century diesel finds Steamtown's restored former Nickel Plate Road GP9, which is often assigned to the daily demonstration excursion, on its way from Cleveland to Buffalo. The old Nickel Plate Road skirted the northwest corner of Pennsylvania, running through the streets of Erie and crossing creeks on tall steel trestles. Perhaps best known for its late use of superpower steam on freight, the railroad was merged with Norfolk & Western in 1964. Brian Solomon

elements of railroading including controversial labor issues, the role of the hobo, women railroaders in a man's world, and discriminatory practices that once existed toward black railroaders.

A mockup of a DL&W ticket office greets prospective passengers, complete with a mannequin ticket agent with a weary scowl. Exhibits covering Amtrak, Conrail, and the effects of deregulation help viewers understand changes in the rail industry during the late twentieth century.

Another wing of the museum is devoted to railroad technology. A hands-on exhibit demonstrates how a steam locomotive valve gear works—a crucial technology that enabled the engineer to govern the power of the locomotive. To help visitors comprehend how a locomotive converted coal and water to rotary power, an actual locomotive has been cut open to expose, highlight, and explain key components normally hidden from sight. The locomotive firebox, boiler tubes, smoke box, pistons, valves, and rods are all laid bare and color coded for added clarity.

Equipment Demonstrated and Displayed

Steamtown wouldn't be Steamtown without its famous collection of locomotives. In addition to static engines displayed on the grounds, a few locomotives are maintained in operable condition and are used for demonstrations and excursions. While steam power is always displayed at the museum, steam locomotives are not necessarily fired up every day (steam locomotives are very costly to maintain and operate, part of the reason they were abandoned in the first place). On some days, vintage diesels operate demonstration trains instead of steam. If you're set on seeing a steam locomotive in action, your best bet is to visit Steamtown on a weekend. The museum also frequently operates short excursions, while at various times it offers longer excursions over the former DL&W main line to Moscow or Tobyhanna for passengers to enjoy.

Among the most interesting sites at Steamtown are the active shops where historic cars and locomotives are maintained, repaired, and restored. The museum is home to one of the few surviving steam-era shops

Canadian coincidences: From the cab of his former Canadian Pacific M-636 diesel-electric, Delaware-Lackawanna engineer Richard Janesko waves to the crew aboard Steamtown's former Canadian Pacific steam locomotive 2317. It is a remarkable coincidence that these two former CPR locomotives work side by side on former DL&W rails at Scranton. Also coincidental is Canadian Pacific's own Scranton operations, which are a function of its 1990 acquisition of the Delaware & Hudson. (A longtime operator in Scranton, D&H acquired the section of the old DL&W between Scranton and Binghamton from Conrail in 1980.) As a result, now CPR's freight trains are regular visitors to Scranton, but back in the steam era, when DL&W ruled Scranton, Canadian Pacific was a long way away. Brian Solomon

Canadian Pacific 2317, as viewed from the cab of a Delaware-Lackawanna Alco-Century diesel rolling westward near the Steamtown Mall. Brian Solomon

This morning view east across the Scranton yards finds a Delaware-Lackawanna freight being switched with a former Lehigh Valley Alco C-420. To the right of the locomotive, the walkway from Steamtown to the mall mimics the angle and alignment of the old DL&W coaling trestle that once occupied the same site. Beyond the walkway is the restored sanding bin and dryer that was built in 1917. It consists of a concrete cylinder that is 50 feet in diameter. In the distance are the old DL&W erecting shops, which are now used to manufacture shell casings for the U.S. Army. Brian Solomon

where visitors can see heavy locomotive work in progress. Tours of the shops are available on a daily basis.

Freight and Passenger Cars

Steam locomotives are the museum's obvious attraction, but among its collection are also restored period freight cars, many of which are more significant to the region than the steam locomotives on display. Among those is the Pennsylvania Railroad boxcar. Once standard and built in the thousands, these cars were part of the landscape for decades. Many—such as PRR No. 109760, built in 1919—were painted in utilitarian rusty brown. Other lines decorated their cars with slogans or advertising.

While this PRR car is made of steel, the first boxcars were made of wood. Later, boxcars had steel frames with wooden sides and ends. A perfect example of this type of car is DL&W 43651, which is exhibited inside the museum. It was among the cars that were sought out, acquired, and thoroughly and authentically restored because it is part of the DL&W's heritage in the region. It was constructed in 1922 at America Car & Foundry in nearby Berwick, Pennsylvania, as a 36-foot-long car built with greater capacity than the older, smaller boxcars it replaced.

Unlike the coal hopper, which was a specialized type of car, the boxcar was intended as the universal vessel for freight transport. The DL&W 43651 was used to move grain from lakeside elevators at Buffalo to Hoboken and to transport cement from DL&W's Bangor and Portland branches in eastern Pennsylvania, among other jobs.

Anthracite, DL&W's lifeblood, moved through Scranton for destinations across the northeast for decades. Although they came and went on a daily basis in the late nineteenth century and early twentieth century, DL&W's omnipresent coal hoppers seemed like part of Scranton's furniture. Today, three representative coal hoppers are displayed on the Steamtown grounds. Each are restored into classic DL&W black livery and on display filled with lumps of anthracite. These cars not only lend the flavor of a period railroad yard, but also allow visitors to get a sense for the size and type of equipment used for hauling coal during the period when DL&W's modern steam shops were developed.

Steamtown also has a number of classic cabooses on display. One of the classic cabooses is DL&W No. 889. Like many cabooses, it rides on a pair of four-wheel trucks, uses all-steel construction, features a centrally positioned elevated cupola—where the conductor or a brakemen might ride to inspect the train and watch for signs of the dreaded hotbox—and sports red paint. Museum visitors can walk through an authentically restored Rutland Railroad caboose inside the museum buildings.

Steamtown's passenger car collection is focused on the steel heavyweight era that began in about 1907 and ran through the mid-1930s, when railroads began acquiring new, flashy streamlined cars. This conscious effort is intended to keep the collection consistent with the time period defined by the DL&W shop buildings. Heavyweight steel cars carried the majority of rail travelers through the 1950s, and some, such as the DL&W suburban electric cars, remained in daily commuter service into the 1980s. Among the most interesting cars on display is an Erie Railroad business car, complete with open-end observation platform and bedrooms, which was used by company executives during inspec-

tion trips of the railroad. It is similar to first-class sleeping cars and parlor cars operated by many railroads in the pre-streamlined era.

Also displayed is a former Louisville & Nashville railway post office car (RPO) that was used to collect, sort, and distribute letters en route. Special bag-snatching and dropping equipment allowed for rapid collection of mail on moving trains. Clerks onboard the cars rapidly sorted letters and put them into bags for distribution. Most RPO services were discontinued in 1967 when the U.S. Post Office shifted the distribution of mail to airlines and highway services.

Infrastructure and Literature
One of the National Park Service's priorities at Steamtown is to preserve and restore the site's original railroad structures. The classic sanding tower near the shops and the Mattes Street signal tower east of the

The Steamtown complex occupies a portion of the former Delaware, Lackawanna & Western yards and shops at Scranton. Genesee Valley Transportation, parent to the short line called Delaware-Lackawanna, provides freight service over the same routes used by Steamtown's excursions. This provides an interesting mix of historic equipment. On a summer morning before Steamtown visitors arrive, GVT's former New York Central Alco-built RS-32 switches the yard against a backdrop of former Central Railroad of New Jersey and DL&W all-steel passenger cars. Brian Solomon

Steamtown shops and along the old DL&W main line have been recently restored to near their original appearance. Patrick McKnight, who wrote a report about Steamtown's historic structures, notes that the signal tower is typical of those built by DL&W in 1911. It follows a standard plan, and it is constructed of concrete, which it makes characteristic of a DL&W structure from the Truesdale period. As explained later, Lackawanna became a showcase for reinforced concrete construction under Truesdale.

As one of several switch towers in Scranton, it was a dynamic focal point for railroad operations. It was used to direct and authorize train movements at the east end of the yard, now occupied by Steamtown, and through the passenger station from the time of its construction until the tower closed in 1953. Like most switch towers,

it was manned by skilled operators 24 hours a day, seven days a week. A state-of-the-art electro-pneumatic plant used bursts of compressed air to move switch points. DL&W's state-of-the-art color light signals, some of which date from the same period as the tower, are part of the line managed by Steamtown. These, like the tower, are preserved as part of the site. The tower can be seen from Steamtown's daily excursion trains, as well as from the parking lot of the former DL&W passenger station. Tours of the tower are available by appointment and on special occasions.

Lackawanna County Electric City Trolley Station and Museum

Located at the Steamtown complex, Lackawanna County Electric City Trolley Station and Museum is

Although it never operated in Pennsylvania, Steamtown's massive Union Pacific Big Boy remains one of the site's greatest attractions. Built in 1941 by Alco in Schenectady, New York, it was one of 25 Big Boys built for Union Pacific. The total weight of the locomotive is approximately 1.2 million pounds. With its tender, it measures 132 feet, 9.25 inches long. Big Boys operated throughout the 1950s, and this one was officially retired in 1962. It is one of eight extant examples. Brian Solomon

Steamtown's cutaway locomotive reveals the machine's inner workings that are normally hidden from view. Here, the cylinder and valves have been exposed to make it possible to track the path of the steam as it works to power the engine. The valve is on top; it slides back and forth, alternatively admitting steam to one side of the cylinder and then the other, thus forcing the piston back and forth. The engine is designed to be double acting, so the piston is powered on both strokes. Brian Solomon

Inside the workshop at the Lackawanna County Electric City Trolley Station and Museum rests interurban electric car No. 801. It was built by the Jewett Car Company in 1912 and served between Allentown and Philadelphia on Lehigh Valley Transit. Brian Solomon

dedicated to preserving the spirit and artifacts of the age of urban and interurban electric railways in eastern Pennsylvania. This two-faceted experience educates and promotes historical interest in the region's electric railways, while also providing an exhilarating historic trolley ride.

The electric street railway evolved from an earlier era of horse-drawn trams. In 1887, Scranton was the first city in Pennsylvania to adopt this new urban transport system, which led to Scranton being known as Electric City. In Scranton, as in most American cities, the era of electric trolley cars preceded that of widespread use of electricity in the home. In many places, street railways were also the local electric power utility.

A direct outgrowth of the electric street railway was the interurban electric railway, which blended electric trolley car technologies and traditional railway practices to connect urban centers on newly constructed light railway lines. Interurban railways typically used their own rights-of-way outside city centers while sharing trackage with streetcars in cities and towns. Their cars often had a heavier design and were capable of greater speeds than their urban cousins. Interurban railways typically handled freight traffic as well.

By the 1920s, most interurban railways were in decline, yet a few lines in Pennsylvania lasted until the early 1950s. Likewise, street railways were largely abandoned as automobile usage increased during the first half of the twentieth century. However, in Philadelphia and Pittsburgh, parts of their extensive streetcar systems have been retained for public transit, with some lines extending into the nearby suburbs.

The museum has preserved roughly 30 examples of electric railway vehicles, of which about a dozen have been restored for display or operation. Among the

Among the locomotives displayed at Steamtown is this historic Electro-Motive Corporation diesel-electric built as DL&W No. 426 in 1935 as part of a preproduction order for two diesel-electric switchers. It was among EMC's first diesel switchers, and it was assembled under contract at General Electric's Erie Plant. In later years, it worked for Bethlehem Steel's Patapsco & Back Rivers line. The locomotive was since purchased by the Genesee Valley Transportation subsidiary Delaware-Lackawanna railroad, and it has been repainted and renumbered to resemble its appearance as built. It is displayed by Steamtown in Scranton. This is one of only a few surviving DL&W locomotives; it is several years older than some of the steam locomotives on display. Scott R. Snell

more interesting pieces displayed are Philadelphia & Western car Nos. 46 and 401, both examples of heavy interurban electrics built by the St. Louis Car Company in 1907. Typical of wooden-body interurban cars of the period, these cars have a style that is equated with the late Victorian and Edwardian eras and feature elegant arched windows.

So why would a Philadelphia area electric line buy cars from St. Louis when the J. G. Brill Company, America's largest trolley car manufacturer, was on its doorstep? The fact that the St. Louis Car Company's president had close financial ties to P&W didn't hurt. This well-known electric railway was one of several interurban lines in Pennsylvania that used heavy third-rail electrification instead of the more common overhead wire. It connected Upper Darby at Philadelphia's city line with Norristown over its own right-of-way, and it eventually evolved into a rapid transit-like operation, which made it unique in the annals of Pennsylvania electric lines.

Until the 1950s, the Lehigh Valley Transit trolley-operated interurban ran over its tracks at Norristown, with cars from Allentown. Unlike virtually all the electric

interurban systems in the United States, most of the P&W trackage remains an active transit line today and is now SEPTA Route 100. In the early 1930s, when many interurbans were in their death throes, P&W invested in a fleet of specially designed double-ended streamlined lightweight cars for its Norristown services. Known for their aerodynamic profile and rapid acceleration, these became known as bullet cars and served for six decades. P&W car No. 206, built in 1931 by Brill in Philadelphia, is one of the surviving P&W bullets.

Among the streetcars in the museum's collection are several Philadelphia Suburban Transit trolley cars, which worked former West Chester Traction Company lines west of the 69th Street Terminal at Upper Darby (remaining portions are still operated by SEPTA to Media and Sharon Hill). Old PST Car No. 80 is a Brill master unit, a relatively late-era lightweight trolley car that worked for a full five decades in daily service and is among the working cars in the museum's fleet. Another car regularly operated at Scranton is PST 76, a large center door–type streetcar built by Brill for West Chester Traction Company. It is among one of the few classic heavy streetcars remaining in service in Pennsylvania.

Visitors to the museum get to experience one of the best preserved electric lines in the state. Electric cars routinely operate on more than five miles of a section of the old Laurel Line, which opened in 1903 and was traditionally operated by the Lackawanna and Wyoming Valley. This 19-mile, third-rail electric railway connected Scranton, Pittston, and Wilkes-Barre to carry both freight and passengers. In its heyday, high-speed Laurel Line electric cars operated every 30 minutes and took 33 to 38 minutes to complete their run.

Today, passengers board restored electric cars from a platform that is adjacent to that used by Steamtown's passenger trains. During the 11-mile round trip, passengers are treated to a symphony of sounds associated with early electric railways. After everyone is on board, the distinctive "ding ding" signals the motorman, who operates the car, to proceed. Other bells ring as the conductor accounts for fares. The old 650-volt third-rail electrification was removed in the early 1950s; an exhibit in the museum explains the details of the third-rail system. Today, cars are powered by the more common overhead wire electrification that was installed as part of the line's restoration a few years ago. Motors below the car use their power to propel the cars forward from a standstill. As the motorman steps up power to the motors, you will hear a distinct rise in the pitch of the whirring below the floor.

Delaware-Lackawanna M636 3643, known to crews as "Loretta," works the yard at the Steamtown complex in Scranton at the restored Mattes Street Tower. The DL&W's early twentieth-century modernization was a showcase for reinforced concrete. Not only was this material used in the construction of its famous bridges, but it was also used in its stations, towers, and other structures.
Patrick Yough

The Lackawanna County Electric City Trolley Station and Museum occupies buildings on the site of the old Dickson Locomotive machine shops and is part of the Steamtown site. Several restored electric trolley cars and interurbans are displayed here, along with artifacts relating to electric transport history. Car 401 was built by the St. Louis Car Company for the Philadelphia & Western. Brian Solomon

The trolley ride at the station is one of the best in the country. It runs over nearly six miles of the former Laurel Line third-rail electric route. Today, this ride is operated with overhead trolley wire and includes sections of line just reopened after years of dormancy. Here, Philadelphia Suburban Transportation Co. No. 76 bursts forth from the gloomy confines of the famous Crown Avenue Tunnel on its outward run from Scranton. At one time, Laurel Line third-rail electrics ran between Scranton and Wilkes-Barre at speeds faster than one can legally drive a car between the two cities today. Brian Solomon

The first few hundred feet of the trolley line are on the grounds of the DL&W shops. After the trolley passes the old erecting shop, it joins the alignment of the traditional Laurel Line. Opposite the DL&W station on a lower level, the Laurel Line once maintained its own passenger terminal, complete with turning loop. As the car rattles forward and the line descends into the valley, you'll notice the old Delaware, Lackawanna & Western main line on a higher level on the right. Those tracks are used by Steamtown's excursion trains and freights. It is not unusual to spot a Steamtown shuttle working this line as the trolley winds its way along.

The highlight of the trolley ride is the reopened, old Crown Avenue Tunnel below Moosic Mountain in Scranton. The car plunges into darkness as it hurdles through the long tunnel. The tunnel was abandoned for many years until the trolley line was rebuilt a few years ago. Adjusting one's eyes after emerging into daylight may take a few moments. Although it is a regular tourist attraction, this remnant of the Laurel Line is more than just a trolley ride. As the car winds along, it passes junctions with freight lines that are still used to tap local industry.

Visiting Steamtown

Since there are no intercity passenger rail services to Scranton, visitors arrive by road. The fastest way to Steamtown is to take the Central Scranton Expressway from Interstate 81—the north-south corridor that bisects the region—and follow signs to Lackawanna Avenue, which runs parallel to the old DL&W in the downtown. This route passes the majestic former DL&W main passenger station, which now serves as a Radisson Hotel. Steamtown's entrance is off Lackawanna Avenue, west of the mall. The road goes beneath the old DL&W Bridge 60 and loops into the old shop complex.

Posed out front are several static steam locomotives, including Reading Company T-1 4-8-4, No. 2124, which was built at Reading to haul coal in the 1940s. It was a star in Reading Rambles excursions during the 1960s. Also in front is one of Union Pacific's legendary Big Boys—among the largest steam locomotives ever built.

CHAPTER 4

LACKAWANNA HERITAGE

An important part of Steamtown's legacy is the old Delaware, Lackawanna & Western with a fascinating heritage well worth exploration. Although as a company the DL&W is but a memory, visitors to Steamtown will be pleased to see the occasional passing of freight trains on the old Lackawanna main line. These are not a demonstration but are for-profit revenue-earning freight trains operated by Genesee Valley Transportation's Delaware-Lackawanna Railroad. Since 1993, they have operated on three historic routes. The most significant is eastward on the old Delaware, Lackawanna & Western main line, where DL freights share the line with Steamtown excursions, much as the historic DL&W's coal trains shared tracks with its famous *Lackawanna Limited.*

Steamtown rarely operates east of Moscow Station, but DL freights make a round trip eastward over the Poconos through the Delaware Water Gap three days a week to a connection with Norfolk

Southern at Slateford Junction near Portland, Pennsylvania. This is real mountain railroading, and trains usually require two or more diesels to lift tonnage over the old Lackawanna grades.

DL's other lines include service over the Laurel Line to reach industrial parks on the south side of Scranton. They reach the parks via a zigzag switchback line that connects with the Laurel Line. The route requires a freight to reverse direction twice in order to gain the elevation necessary to reach an old line segment once operated by the Erie Railroad. This unusual arrangement is a reflection of the patchwork nature of Scranton's surviving lines, which comprise of portions of competing railway systems in the region. DL also serves portions of the old Delaware & Hudson, both to reach its yards and shops geographically south of Steamtown, while running north toward the historic coal-producing town of Carbondale.

Facing page: At Slateford Junction, the old DL&W line here is being overtaken by nature. Once an important junction where the old main line and the Slateford Cutoff (better known today as the New Jersey Cutoff) came together, this tower was the operations center that controlled the switches and signals. Now it is only a concrete shell. The cutoff was abandoned by Conrail in its cost-cutting days. Likewise, the old main line has been severed. Delaware-Lackawanna still maintains an interchange with Norfolk Southern here. NS runs a local out of Allentown to deliver and collect freight cars. It is hoped that someday the cutoff may be reopened and through passenger service will be restored. Brian Solomon

Above: The old DL&W station at Cresco has been recently restored. It is one of several nicely preserved structures along the old DL&W main line in Pennsylvania, and it is located on the east slope of Pocono Summit. Brian Solomon

A few miles east of Scranton near Elmhurst, Delaware-Lackawanna's tri-weekly through freight to Slateford Junction climbs eastward. It travels along Roaring Brook and toward Pocono Summit on the former Delaware, Lackawanna & Western main line. Under the progressive Truesdale administration, between 1902 and 1908, DL&W installed three main-line tracks on its grade over Pocono Summit. The purpose of the tracks was to allow fast freight and passenger trains to overtake slow-moving coal drags without impeding traffic. During the Conrail era, the line was severed as a through route, automatic block signaling was discontinued, and all but one of the tracks was taken out of service. Today, the railroad is essentially preserved as part of the Steamtown site—complete with the old signal bridges—while DL provides freight service. Brian Solomon

DL is among a few railroads that still assign old Alco diesels to through freight service. Therefore, DL is a popular line with railroad enthusiasts. Alco exited the domestic locomotive market in 1969, while its Canadian affiliate Montreal Locomotive Works (MLW) continued to build similar machines for a few more years. DL's Alco fleet consists of many different Alco and MLW models acquired over the years from other railroads. DL maintains its active Alcos at its Scranton shops where a number of derelict locomotives

are stored. Some of the old locomotives serve as the railroad's parts supply, and others await a call to duty that may someday see them working freight trains for this colorful regional line.

Some of DL's Alco diesels are as historic as the steam locomotives at Steamtown. Among them are two of the last serviceable as-built model RS3s. There were more than 1,300 RS3s built between 1950 and 1956 to replace steam on railroads all across North America. In Pennsylvania, RS3s were used by Delaware-Lackawanna,

PHOEBE SNOW

Early in the twentieth century, DL&W launched a legendary advertising campaign to promote both its new luxury passenger service *Lackawanna Limited* and the benefits of anthracite coal. The campaign featured the character of Phoebe Snow—a fictional young woman of pale complexion who dressed in white and traveled frequently from New York to Buffalo.

Phoebe Snow was created to mirror the qualities of anthracite coal—a fuel source that produced relatively little ash and soot. Because DL&W's locomotives consumed it and its hoppers carried thousands of tons of anthracite to market daily, Phoebe implied that anthracite was ideal for the home because of its clean-burning attributes. Posters and magazine ads featured the spotless Phoebe—in real life a model named Marion Murray—posed in innumerable railroad situations normally associated with grime and filth. Each ad was accompanied by a clever rhyming slogan themed around both DL&W services and anthracite coal. The most famous and oft repeated of these is:

> "Says Phoebe Snow
> About to go
> Upon a trip
> To Buffalo
> My gown stays white
> From morn till night
> Upon the Road of Anthracite."

Dozens of such ditties were composed over the years. Among the more obscure is the message below, emphasizing the safety of Lackawanna's new signaling system. In the early 1900s, at a time when horrendous rear-end accidents sparked a sense of peril for many railway travelers, this theme elevated DL&W's concern for safety above that of other lines:

> "Devoid of fear
> With roadbed clear
> The engineer
> Notes green and white
> Of signal light
> 'Tis the safe Road
> Of Anthracite."

(In those days, a white light represented clear, while green was used for caution.)

The original Phoebe Snow campaign ended around World War I. However, in 1949, on the 50th anniversary of the inauguration of the *Lackawanna Limited*, DL&W debuted its new Hoboken-to-Buffalo streamliner, christened *The Phoebe Snow*. The train operated into the Erie Lackawanna era but was finally cancelled a few years before the advent of Amtrak. By that time, the old Lackawanna was no longer a through route to Buffalo. Its lines had been merged with those of Erie, and much of its original route west of Binghamton had been abandoned.

Over the years and even into the twenty-first century, Phoebe Snow generated intense public interest in Lackawanna. She remains a celebrity today, more than a century after she first appeared and decades after the Lackawanna and its passenger trains faded from the scene.

Central Railroad of New Jersey, Erie Railroad, Lehigh Valley, Pennsylvania Railroad, Reading Company, and Western Maryland, among other lines.

Delaware-Lackawanna is a silent player in the Steamtown excursions. It maintains and operates the lines that Steamtown operates its trains on and qualifys the site's locomotive crews. DL's operations are located at Bridge 60—which carries the old DL&W line across the valley and above the former D&H tracks that DL's freight trains use to reach the tracks at Steamtown. As the result of careful dispatching, Steamtown and DL can safely share the same tracks. The track share allows the lines to serve as both a popular excursion route and revenue freight corridor in the Scranton area.

Visiting DL&W's Tunkhannock and Martins Creek Viaducts

The Summit Cutoff line between Scranton and Binghamton is one of the few segments of the DL&W main line still used daily as a through freight route operated by the Canadian Pacific, which also hosts Norfolk Southern trains. Typically, the bridge sees four to eight though freights daily. The timings of these trains depend on a host of variables, so it's difficult to predict when they will soar across the valley on DL&W's classic viaducts.

Under Erie Lackawanna, the old DL&W main line east of Binghamton, New York, was a favored freight route. On August 17, 1971, more than a dozen years before Steamtown began its relocation to Scranton, Steamtown's former Nickel Plate Road Berkshire-type No. 759 hauled Erie Lackawanna westward revenue freight over Pocono Summit. This ferry move was necessary to get the locomotive back to Bellows Falls, Vermont, where Steamtown was based at that time. It is seen here passing the yet-to-be restored station at Cresco, Pennsylvania. George W. Kowanski

The view from the cab of the second unit on Delaware-Lackawanna's westward freight PT97 shows it charging westward in the rain through the famous Delaware Water Gap. Once the route of DL&W's famous Lackawanna Limited *and its 1949 streamliner* The Phoebe Snow, *the line through the Water Gap is now mostly used for freight service.* Brian Solomon

Driving northwest of Scranton on Highway 11, you approach the village of Nicholson, Pennsylvania, on a well-graded road that is the original DL&W right-of-way. As you round the bend to cross Tunkhannock Creek, DL&W's colossal neo-Roman Tunkhannock Viaduct looms above and spans the entire valley. Nearly a half-mile long (2,375 feet), it rises 240 feet over the valley floor to tower over the houses and shops in the village. The viaduct was the largest reinforced-concrete bridge in the world when it was completed in 1915.

The scale of the bridge dwarfs that of the trains that cross it. Observers from ground level are often surprised when, from their perspective, they see a "tiny" train inch across the bridge. The structure's high parapets compound this problem for photographers. The bridge is part of the Summit Cutoff, Truesdale's line change that significantly reduced the gradient and the curvature on the tough mountain crossing. It also cut 3.6 miles off the old route and now is used in part by Highway 11.

This bridge, like DL&W's other concrete viaducts, was a showcase for reinforced concrete construction and largely the work of the railroad's bridge engineer Abraham Burton Cohen. Tunkhannock consists of 10 enormous arched spans that are each 180 feet long. An estimated 167,000 cubic yards of concrete and an estimated 1,140 tons of steel were used in its construction. DL&W's engineers kept track of progress during construction by using detailed drawings to represent the volume of concrete in place.

By continuing north on Highway 11, you will come to a similar bridge over Martins Creek, which spans the road as well. This bridge is slightly shorter than Tunkhannock but was built for three tracks. It only carries one track today.

The old DL&W main line passes through the edge of Nay Aug Park on the northeast side of Scranton. Twin tunnels here once hosted four tracks back in the days when the Lackawanna was a heavy freight and passenger route. Now, just one main track and a rarely used siding remain. Delaware-Lackawanna M636, No. 3643, descends westward through the Nay Aug Tunnel with symbol freight PT97 on a frigid winter afternoon. A parallel portal, out of sight to the right, is abandoned. Scott R. Snell

After finishing his run from Scranton to Slateford Junction and back, Delaware-Lackawanna engineer Mike Vassallo leaves the pair of RS3s that he has worked with for most of the day. He and conductor Dave Heller worked the better part of 12 hours on the old Delaware, Lackawanna & Western; they are keeping the spirit of railroading alive on the rails over Pocono Summit. Brian Solomon

Rolling west toward the setting sun, Delaware-Lackawanna RS3 4103 approaches the old Delaware, Lackawanna & Western passenger station with freight PT97 from Slateford Junction. It has been many years since passengers arrived in Scranton by train from distant stations. When this magnificent building was completed in 1908, it was part of a large-scale upgrade of DL&W's lines and facilities. It remains an important Scranton landmark. Brian Solomon

The Delaware Water Gap was one of the most famous locations on the old Delaware, Lackawanna & Western. It was used to pose the famous Phoebe Snow *streamliner for publicity photos. Through the 1950s, DL&W operated eight to 10 through freights in each direction daily, plus a complement of passenger trains. Today, the tri-weekly Delaware-Lackawanna freights to and from Scranton keep the rails polished.* Brian Solomon

DL&W's open-spandrel concrete Tunkhannock Creek Viaduct was the most significant piece of new infrastructure on its Summit Cutoff. The bridge is seen here near completion on June 26, 1915. As the bridge was built, its engineers carefully gauged their progress using profile-view blueprints that showed the level concrete in place. Today, the right-of-way of the old line at Nicholson—seen here with an eastward passenger train crossing the creek—serves as Highway 11. Photo by Bunnell, Syracuse University via Thomas T. Taber collection, Railroad Museum of Pennsylvania PHMC

Less photographed than its larger cousin, Lackawanna's Martins Creek Viaduct is located just a few miles compass north of Nicholson. It shares the same essential characteristics with the Tunkhannock Viaduct. A southward Norfolk Southern autorack (enclosed car for moving new automobiles) freight crosses the bridge heading for Enola Yards near Harrisburg by way of Scranton. This view was captured on a May afternoon from a country road on the opposite side of the valley from the bridge. Route 11 passes directly below the bridge. Brian Solomon

CHAPTER 5

JIM THORPE AND THE LEHIGH GORGE

The rise of the automobile devastated tourism in the Lehigh Valley. Whereas Mauch Chunk was conveniently situated on two main lines—Lehigh Valley Railroad and Central Railroad of New Jersey served the town via opposite banks of the Lehigh River—it was off the beaten path for highway travelers. As passenger train travel waned after World War II, so did tourism to Mauch Chunk. On top of that, the anthracite that spurred the town's boom was no longer the fuel of choice. These factors further impacted Mauch Chunk's once-prosperous economy and forced the town to find another way to attract visitors by renaming itself Jim Thorpe (see the related sidebar later in this chapter).

CNJ, which had once promoted travel to the town, abandoned most passenger services in the region in the 1950s. Yet, it continued to operate suburban services in New Jersey until it was included in Conrail in 1976. Lehigh Valley, once legendary for its famed *Black Diamond*, ended all of its passenger services on February 3, 1961. It was one of the first large railroads in the east to completely give up on passenger traffic. While CNJ's elegant 1888-built passenger station remains a key fixture in Jim Thorpe, the old Lehigh Valley station is just a memory. A few of the roads' tracks remain on both sides of the Lehigh River at Jim Thorpe.

On the east bank, the old Lehigh Valley line remains part of a moderately busy freight corridor. It was served in 2007 by Norfolk Southern and Canadian Pacific via trackage rights, with four to six freights using the line every day. The west bank hosts tracks of the old Central Railroad of New Jersey. While no longer a through route to Jersey City, portions of this line are used by modern-day regional railroad Reading & Northern as part of its network of lines in eastern Pennsylvania.

Facing page: Reading & Northern provides locomotives and crews for the Lehigh Gorge Scenic Railway excursions that operate on its tracks. Most excursions depart from the old Central Railroad of New Jersey passenger station in historic Jim Thorpe. The locomotive pictured here is an Electro-Motive Division SD50 that was built for heavy freight service in the 1980s. Locomotives are positioned at both ends of excursion trains to simplify operations. Brian Solomon

Above: The Lehigh Gorge is steeped in railroad and industrial history. At Glen Onoko, the older Central Railroad of New Jersey alignment punched through the ridge and crossed the Lehigh River on a bridge beginning at the mouth of the tunnel. This route was later abandoned in favor of an alignment directly adjacent to the Lehigh Valley's line. The old tunnel may be seen from the right side of the train as it winds its way up the gorge from Jim Thorpe. Brian Solomon

R&N hosts weekend passenger excursions through the Lehigh Gorge that are operated by the Lehigh Gorge Scenic Railway and originate at the old CNJ station in Jim Thorpe. These tend to run midday on summer and autumn weekends. A typical round trip into the gorge takes just under an hour, and it is well worth the nominal fare. Occasionally, longer trips are offered. The cars that passengers ride in are all-steel former Delaware, Lackawanna & Western suburban equipment and are hauled by relatively modern Reading & Northern freight diesels (in 2007 these were General Motors Electro-Motive Division SD50s). There are no turning facilities at the end of the excursion run, so passenger consists typically operate a locomotive at both ends.

The route these passenger excursions follow is the R&N line north (old railroad-direction west) from Jim Thorpe. After heading out of the station, passengers can see a variety of stored historical railroad equipment in the old CNJ yard on the left side of the train. Beyond the yard, the excursion train heads to the right at Nesquehoning Junction. Here, R&N's freight-only C&S branch diverges from the old CNJ main line. Despite the decline of anthracite, R&N still moves

some hard coal over this line. CNJ's derelict, old interlocking tower that once controlled train movements through the junction sits on the left side of the line.

After the tracks curve sharply to the right, they cross the Lehigh River on a heavy plate girder deck bridge and then span the former Lehigh Valley Railroad on a steel truss. Both bridges originally carried double track that dates to when CNJ was a major anthracite hauler. On the east bank of the Lehigh River, the old Lehigh Valley and Central Railroad of New Jersey lines ran adjacent to one another for many miles in the narrow confines of the gorge. Today, after crossing the river, both the Reading & Northern and Norfolk Southern tracks run parallel on the former Lehigh Valley align-

Jim Thorpe is famous for its well preserved and eclectic Victorian architecture. Keeping in line with the community is the former Central Railroad of New Jersey station on the eastern edge of downtown, on the corner of Susquehanna and Broadway. Built back in 1888, when Jim Thorpe was still Mauch Chunk, this station is known for its distinctive three-story tower and conical roof. While regularly scheduled, long-distance passenger trains last called here in the 1950s, the station is now used by passengers of the Lehigh Gorge Scenic Railway to embark on hour-long railroad excursions. Brian Solomon

The Lehigh Gorge Scenic Railway offers seasonal weekend and holiday train rides through the Lehigh Scenic Gorge State Park. The train uses a blend of former Central Railroad of New Jersey and Lehigh Valley Railroad lines, starting from the old CNJ station in Jim Thorpe. Beyond Glen Onoko, excursions follow the former LV route, while the old CNJ line that serves as a bike trail runs on a parallel alignment. Brian Solomon

FROM MAUCH CHUNK TO JIM THORPE

When the decline of the anthracite industry and passenger rail service hit Mauch Chunk hard in the early 1950s, residents believed something must be done to keep people coming to this once popular tourist destination.

In 1954, they made the unorthodox decision to rename the town in honor of the famous athlete Jim Thorpe (he had no prior connection to the area). They felt the move could attract attention and boost tourism.

Jim Thorpe (1887–1953) was among America's most renowned athletes in the first half of the twentieth century. Part Native American (of the Sac and Fox tribe) and part Irish, he was an outstanding football and baseball player. He also competed in the 1912 Olympics and won several Olympic medals. The medals were later stripped from him because of his role in professional sports.

While many residents still refer to the town of Jim Thorpe by its traditional name (Mauch Chunk, which means Mountain of Sleeping Bear or Bear Mountain), the town has revived its tourism business. Many of the town's original Victorian buildings survive, and it is home to a number of interesting railway sites. Among the places worth visiting is the Asa Packer Mansion, once home to Lehigh Valley Railroad's visionary promoter.

For anyone who is curious to learn more about Jim Thorpe—the town and the man—visit the Mauch Chunk Museum and Cultural Center. Located on the west side of town in an old red brick Methodist church, it is about a 10-minute walk from the Central Railroad of New Jersey station. A nominal donation is accepted. Exhibits include a short and very informative documentary film; a host of artifacts; and displays relating to the mining of coal, canals, and railroads in the area, as well as an interpretive model of the old Switchback gravity railroad.

Today, on Opera House Square and around the corner from the vintage venue, is a railroad-themed photography gallery, the Gandy Dancer. Run by a retired railroader, the gallery is full of reasonably priced vintage and contemporary railroad images that feature a variety of streamlined passenger trains and locomotives from the 1930s and 1940s.

ment, while the old CNJ alignment serves as a road and bicycle trail through the gorge. Near Glen Onoko, both alignments cross to the west bank. From the right side of the train, the remnants of an old CNJ tunnel can be seen in the rock wall of the gorge.

As the train winds up through the gorge, it passes the famous Oxbow Bend. The location now known as Independence, near old Penn Haven Junction, is as far as most excursions travel. Beyond this point, the two tracks join. As discussed by Robert F. Archer in his *A History of the Lehigh Valley Railroad*, this was once the location of inclined planes operated by the Hazelton Railroad. The station building that once stood here was only accessible by rail, since no roads reached this far up the Lehigh Gorge.

Visiting Jim Thorpe

Jim Thorpe is on Pennsylvania State Route 209 (which can be easily reached via Pennsylvania Turnpike Extension I-476, about 45 minutes south of Scranton and less than two hours from Philadelphia). On the way into town, Route 209 passes the classic CNJ station with its three-story round tower and distinctive conical roof. Metered parking is available in front of the station. All-day paid parking is open across the tracks, just north of the station.

Preserved first-generation diesels often can be seen parked north of the station. Inside the building is a tourist office and exhibits relating to the area's railroads. Displayed in a small park adjacent to the station is an enormous slab of anthracite taken from the Mammoth vein.

Jim Thorpe also offers an array of excellent hiking or bicycling options. Visitors to Glen Onoko State Park can cycle along the former Central Railroad of New Jersey line through the Lehigh Gorge, which is adjacent to the route of the Lehigh Gorge Scenic Railway and Norfolk Southern tracks described above. The park, which is just across the river, has several parking areas. To reach the narrow confines of the gorge, the best

From the ridgeline near Glen Onoko, and looking timetable-west and compass north up the Lehigh River Gorge, an excursion train is seen crossing the Lehigh River on the former Lehigh Valley Railroad alignment. The adjacent bridge is a later alignment used by the Central Railroad of New Jersey, which now carries a road into the park. Brian Solomon

Near Nesquehoning Junction, Reading & Northern SD50 5014 leads an excursion across the former Central Railroad of New Jersey bridge over the Lehigh River toward Jim Thorpe. This trackage had been out of service since CNJ retrenched from its Pennsylvania operations in 1972 when R&N restored it to service in late 2003. Scott R. Snell

place to park is near the old CNJ bridge on the west bank. From here, you can ride or hike up to Oxbow Bend, named for the sharp turn in the river, where company photographers would pose the *Black Diamond* on its way to and from Buffalo.

For those interested in a walking tour, The Switchback Gravity Railroad Foundation (which has an office upstairs in the CNJ station) has published a detailed walking route map of the old Switchback lines. The map shows both up and down routes between Jim Thorpe and the old mines at Summit Hill. Many sections of the old Switchback have been cleared and give visitors a sense for what this amazing early railway was like.

Another interesting rail site can be seen west of Jim Thorpe on Road 3012, heading toward Summit Hill. Several miles out of town on the left is Mauch Chunk Lake Park. Near the entrance, the right-of-way of down track of the Mauch Chunk Gravity Railroad crosses Road 3012. Just east of the entrance, in the trees, the line has been cleared and short sections of track were reconstructed with a replica of a Switchback car spotted for all to see.

For the most spectacular view of Jim Thorpe, drive east of town on Route 209, take a left on Beaver Run

Road, and follow the signs to Flagstaff, a restaurant with a viewing area at the edge of the gorge. From here, the CNJ railroad station and yards are clearly visible, as well as the Asa Packer mansion with its red roof. In autumn and winter, when the trees are without leaves, you are treated to a clear view of the former Lehigh Valley main line. From this vantage point, you just might be lucky enough to see an occasional freight train snaking its way through the gorge.

Visiting Pioneer Tunnel Coal Mine

Another interesting rail site in this area where mining, the moving of coal, and the railroad were intertwined is the Pioneer Tunnel Coal Mine in Ashland, Pennsylvania (36 miles southwest of Jim Thorpe). Here, the mine's colliery—the railway that transported coal from the mine to the surface and from the mine opening to where the coal was crushed, sorted, and separated from other material—has been revived, but wholly as a tourist operation. The site offers visitors a rare look at the type of rail operations that first developed in this country and led to the evolution of modern railroading.

Reopened in 1962, the Pioneer Tunnel Coal Mine has the veneer of a period roadside attraction, but that shouldn't dissuade visitors from taking the time to explore this aspect of railroading.

Two rides are offered. The first and more interesting ride uses a battery-operated mining motor to haul passengers over roughly laid track, deep into the old mine once operated by the Philadelphia & Reading Coal & Iron Company, a coal mining affiliate of the Reading Company. These 42-inch gauge tracks and unsprung mining cars were built to haul coal, not people, so the ride into the mine is a bone-shaking experience.

Inside the mine, temperatures average a cool 52 degrees, and passengers can view veins of anthracite in the dimly lit tunnel as the cars rattle along. Shafts blasted into the veins of coal pitch up and down at 55-degree angles from the level passages, reflecting the natural angle of the veins. The guides give detailed explanations of how this coal was extracted and how the region's anthracite mining boom affected technology, business, politics, and the community in the surrounding area. Guides also talk about the immigrants from Ireland, Wales, and Eastern Europe who toiled in this mine and many other mines like it to extract "black diamonds." Immigrants worked in dangerous conditions because the threat of poisonous gases, tunnel collapses, and eventually black lung disease was constant.

The other ride is entirely outdoors. A tiny 0-4-0 industrial saddle-tank steam locomotive named *Henry Clay*—a nineteenth-century politician and one-time presidential candidate—built by the Vulcan Iron Works of Wilkes-Barre in 1927 is used to move cart loads of passengers. This short rail line was built to move anthracite from the mine opening to a nearby breaker. The tracks are contiguous with those inside the mine. When this was a going enterprise, mules were employed to haul the loaded mine wagons out of the mine, and locomotives hauled the wagons to the breakers. The tracks both inside and outside of the mine had to be rebuilt when the site was adapted into a museum, since more than 30 years had passed from when it had functioned as a commercial mine.

The ride offers views of Ashland and the mountain scenery around the town, much of which reveals the scars from years of mining. At the end of the line, once the location of the breaker, the tracks of the old Reading Company are clearly visible in the valley below. This section is one of several lines now operated by Reading & Northern, a Conrail-era spinoff that is still earning revenue from the haulage of anthracite.

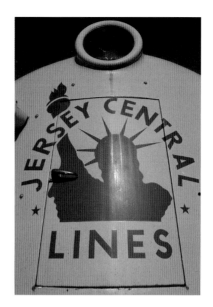

The Central Railroad of New Jersey herald on an old Electro-Motive F3A diesel-electric that has been preserved by the Anthracite Historical Society, near the old CNJ station at Jim Thorpe. Scott Snell

Pioneer Tunnel Coal Mine locomotive No. 1 is named after politician Henry Clay. This 42-inch-gauge locomotive is kept in steam to haul short excursions on the restored industrial railway at Ashland, Pennsylvania. The Vulcan Iron Works was once one of several locomotive builders in Pennsylvania. According to Alfred W. Bruce's The Steam Locomotive in American, *Vulcan built more than 4,000 locomotives between 1874 and 1950 and focused its locomotive production on small industrial types, such as the 0-4-0 pictured here.* Brian Solomon

PART II

PHILADELPHIA AND PENNSYLVANIA DUTCH COUNTRY

During the nineteenth century, Philadelphia developed a dense network of railway lines. While the earliest routes were intended as conveyors of anthracite, the Philadelphia & Columbia—a component of the Main Line of Public Works—was designed as a gateway to the West. By the late nineteenth century, the two major steam railroads in the area—the Pennsylvania Railroad and Philadelphia & Reading—had constructed parallel and competing networks across southeastern Pennsylvania focused on Philadelphia and its port. In addition to the movement of freight, these increasingly developed suburban passenger routes, which, for the first time, enabled workers to live outside city and commute to their places of employment.

Toward the end of the nineteenth century, vast opulent Center City terminals were constructed to accommodate the rising tide of passengers. In the city itself, a dense network of electric trolley lines was built along with elevated and underground rapid transit lines. Initially, these were privately run. Electricity was soon harnessed for the commuter lines, and both PRR and Reading electrified their suburban lines. Although scaled back from its heyday in the 1920s, significant portions of the railroad's suburban routes as well as the cores of the old trolley and rapid transit routes are now operated by the South Eastern Pennsylvania Transportation Authority (SEPTA), while Amtrak provides electric long-distance services on the old PRR. Newer stations have largely replaced the nineteenth-century classic terminals.

The region is also host to some of Pennsylvania's most interesting and diverse railway preservation. In the rolling fields of Pennsylvania Dutch country is the old Strasburg Rail Road—transformed from a bankrupt short line into one of America's foremost tourist railways—and the Railroad Museum of Pennsylvania. Across the region are fragments of old Reading Company branch lines that serve variously as short-line freight carriers and tourist lines, while core main lines of the old Reading host freight trains of Norfolk Southern, CSX, and the regional railroad Reading & Northern.

Pennsylvania Railroad set aside key examples of its most successful steam power. Here are two of its most famous types. On the left is K4s Pacific No 3750; it was designed and built at Altoona for heavy passenger work. It was constructed in 1920 and is one of two surviving examples of the type. In its day, the K4s was one of the most recognized locomotives in America and even the subject of a jazz piece. On the right is a massive M1b Mountain No. 6755, a powerful machine built in 1930 for both freight and passenger service. Loved by both enginemen and photographers, the M1b epitomized PRR's locomotive design. Both locomotives operated until the mid-1950s when they were replaced by diesels. Brian Solomon

Amtrak **TRAIN INFORMATION** time

Time	Number	Train	TO	From	Status	Stairway
10:56	174	ACELA REGIONAL	BOSTON	WASHINGTON	30mins LATE	3
11:05	2153	ACELA EXPRESS-R	WASHINGTON	BOSTON	ON TIME	5
11:08	141	ACELA REGIONAL	WASHINGTON	SPRINGFIELD	ON TIME	7
11:40	20	CRESCENT	PHILADELPHIA	NEW ORLEANS	15mins LATE	8
11:46	108	METROLINER-R	NEW YORK	WASHINGTON		
11:48	4613	N.J. TRANSIT	ATLANTIC CITY	PHILADELPHIA	ON TIME	
12:03	184	ACELA REGIONAL	NEW YORK	WASHINGTON	ON TIME	

• DO NOT LEAVE LUGGAGE OR OTHER ITEMS UNATTENDED •
• UNATTENDED ITEMS WILL BE REMOVED BY AMTRAK POLICE •

◆ ClubAcela Behind Stairway One

Information

CHAPTER 6

PHILADELPHIA

Few cities can claim a more intensive relationship with railways than Philadelphia. Pennsylvania's largest metropolitan area, its seat of finance, and largest port, Philadelphia had been the focus of intense railroad building throughout the nineteenth century. Its railroad legacy is multifaceted: It served as headquarters for both the Philadelphia & Reading and the Pennsylvania Railroad. Both companies operated numerous routes to connect the city with points across the commonwealth and the nation. The railroads developed intensive suburban passenger networks that were improved and largely electrified during the early decades of the twentieth century.

To accommodate growing tides of passengers, these railroads built elaborate stations that were among the grandest in the world. To handle an ever increasing flow of freight, they built large yards and freight terminal facilities. The Delaware River waterfront became a major coal and ore port. Philadelphia also was the home of Baldwin, the most productive of America's steam builders. Its streets were graced with an intensive network of electric streetcars, and later these were augmented by both elevated and underground third-rail rapid transit lines.

Decline from Glory

Since its heyday a century ago, Philadelphia's railway network has been transformeded by industrial decline, mergers, and retrenchment. Reading Company fell from grace as its anthracite empire crumbled. PRR, once America's largest transportation company, merged with New York Central and descended into bankruptcy. When the railroads were melded into Conrail in 1976, Philadelphia was selected as Conrail's headquarters and remained so until the railroad was divided between Norfolk Southern and CSX in 1998 and 1999.

During the Conrail period, portions of the old PRR, Reading Company, and other lines reorganized and combined routes to allow for a more effective separation between freight and passenger routes. PRR's premier electrified main lines—the New York–Philadelphia-Washington route and

Facing page: Philadelphia's 30th Street Station is Amtrak's primary facility in the area. It is the third busiest station on Amtrak's nationwide system, behind New York's Penn Station and Washington's Union Station. Completed in 1933, 30th Street Station uses a neo-classical design. The main concourse, pictured here, is 290 feet long, 135 feet wide, with the ceiling 95 feet above the floor—the same height as Reading Terminal's train shed. The main-line tracks are on high-level platforms that can be reached by escalator. SEPTA suburban tracks are on the upper level and adjacent to the concourse. Brian Solomon

Above: On the street in front of the old station, a period clock reminds passersby of both the time and the significance of the magnificent building on Market Street. Brian Solomon

the Philadelphia-Harrisburg Main Line—were variously conveyed to passenger operators, including Amtrak. It was a move that resulted in withdrawal of most through freight services from these lines.

Philadelphia was among the earliest cities to recognize that in order to maintain suburban passenger services, public funding was needed. In 1958, the city set up the Passenger Service Improvement Corporation to provide relief for Reading and PRR commuter operations. Despite early public subsidies, these networks have been trimmed from their peak. Once separate systems, the former Reading and PRR suburban lines were connected via the new Center City Commuter Connection tunnel in November 1984. The tunnel linked the stub end of PRR's underground Suburban Station to a new Market East Station and the tracks that formerly ran into the Reading Terminal (discussed below).

Many of Amtrak's long-distance passenger services run out of the 30th Street Station on former PRR Northeast Corridor routes. Yet, while the South Eastern Pennsylvania Transportation Authority's (SEPTA) lines radiate to a multitude of suburban destinations—including Newark, Delaware, and the Philadelphia International Airport—passengers haven't been able to take a train from Philadelphia all the way to Allentown, Bethlehem, Reading, or Scranton for many years. You can, however, hop on a NJ Transit (NJT) train at the 30th Street Station to get to Atlantic City. You also can buy through tickets on SEPTA for same-platform connections at Trenton, New Jersey, for NJT trains to Penn Station, New York, for far less than Amtrak fares. (One of SEPTA's best-kept secrets is that it offers seniors substantial discounts on its suburban trains and even free rides with a Medicare ID card on its city buses, streetcars, and subways.)

Philadelphia is one of only a few eastern cities that still has significant portions of its traditional streetcar system. These routes are now operated by SEPTA,

The old Philadelphia & Western third-rail high-speed line from 69th Street Terminal in Upper Darby to Norristown survives as SEPTA's No. 100 line. Best known for hosting the 1931-built bullet cars, the route now is home to modern boxy cars built in 1992 and 1993 by manufacturer ABB. One of these is seen here crossing the Schuylkill at Norristown on a clear October afternoon.
Brian Solomon

After years without regular trolley service along Girard Avenue, SEPTA restored its No. 15 route in 2004 and 2005 with rebuilt vintage Presidents' Conference Committee cars. These are painted in a livery similar to that worn by PCCs of the old Philadelphia Transportation Company. An eastward PCC navigates Girard Avenue on an autumn afternoon. Brian Solomon

including the former Red Arrow suburban routes. While a number of trolley lines were curtailed in the 1980s, the city recently restored service to the No. 15 route along Girard Avenue. This line uses historic PCC cars painted like the trolleys that were once operated by the old Philadelphia Traction Company. One way to get a glimpse of this transit system is to take SEPTA's Market-Frankford subway and El line to the 69th Street Terminal. Then ride one of the former Red Arrow suburban trolley lines to Media or Sharon Hill, or catch a modern third-rail car on the former P&W Norristown Highspeed line. At Norristown, you can take a SEPTA R2 commuter train back to Center City.

Reading Terminal

In the 1890s, Philadelphia & Reading invested its anthracite wealth in the construction of one of Pennsylvania's most ornately decorated company head-quarters and passenger terminals. Facing Philadelphia's Market Street, one of downtown's main thoroughfares, Reading Terminal represented an ostentatious display of success, but one that now has benefited citizens and visitors to Philadelphia for more than a century.

Like many large railway terminals of its time, Reading Terminal followed the architectural pattern

Philadelphia was one of two Pennsylvania cities to retain portions of its electric streetcar network. Among the surviving routes is the No. 34 surface subway line, which runs along Baltimore Avenue on the south side of the city. One of SEPTA's 1981-built single-ended Kawasaki trolleys works this service on a damp December evening. Brian Solomon

The Connecting Railway was built in Philadelphia during 1866 and 1867 to provide the Pennsylvania Railroad with a through route across New Jersey toward New York City. This bridge crosses the Schuylkill River east of Zoo Junction—so named because it is adjacent to the Philadelphia Zoo. It is a five-track replacement span built in 1914 and consists of concrete arches that are faced with sandstone to resemble PRR's earlier bridge at this location. Today, this bridge is part of the Northeast Corridor used by Amtrak, SEPTA, and NJ Transit passenger trains. Brian Solomon

established in Britain and perfected at London's St. Pancras station. This pattern features two distinct structures for the head house and train shed. The Reading station architect F. H. Kimball designed the head house to rise nine stories above the street. Its façade is made of pink and white granite, and it is decorated with terra cotta trimmings. Behind the head house is the functional part of the station, an enormous balloon-style train shed—the last surviving North American example—designed and built by Philadelphia's Wilson Brothers. This building rises to a crest of 95 feet above the platform level and extends 509 feet behind the head house along 12th Street. It was designed to cover 13 tracks, 12 of which would serve passenger trains.

Built to replace three earlier downtown passenger stations, Reading Terminal was a vast station, yet not as big as PRR's similarly styled Broad Street Terminal that was located just a few blocks away. Today, the Reading Terminal is dwarfed by a host of larger buildings. Yet, when it was completed in 1893, its Italian Renaissance style façade seemed gigantic to people on the street.

Reading Terminal served as a downtown passenger station for 91 years. At one time, both long-distance

Located just upriver from the former PRR Connecting Railway bridge, this former Reading Company bridge over the Schuylkill consists of five graceful, concrete elliptical arches. It is used by through freights serving Philadelphia, such as this CSX coal train led by a pair of SD70MACs pictured at the end of a clear September afternoon. Brian Solomon

and suburban trains used its platforms. In later days, it hosted only SEPTA commuter trains. The terminal closed as a result of the consolidation of Philadelphia's suburban services on November 6, 1984. Its modern underground replacement, the new Market East Station, is located not far from it.

The train shed survives and was renovated in 1994 as part of the Pennsylvania Convention Center that opened in 1998. Escalators to the old track level allow visitors to view the immense space of the old shed that is now sanitized and brightly lit for its new function. Murals depict the station as it would have appeared in the steam era, including images of Reading Company's Budd-built steam-hauled *Crusader* streamliner. The train ran directly from its platforms to Central Railroad of New Jersey's Jersey City Terminal in the shadow of the Statue of Liberty. The convention center also has a variety of displays that focus on PRR's history, detailing

its famous T-1 Northern-type steam locomotives, the station's unique architectural features, and the Reading Company's role as an anthracite and iron mining business and a railroad.

Below the old track level is the Reading Terminal Market, which dates from 1893. The market is a carry-over from traditional farmer's markets held near the site from the early 1800s. Today, visitors can enjoy freshly prepared food from a variety of vendors and purchase everything from fresh bread and seafood to exotic imported cheeses, oils, and wine. The Reading Terminal Market retains a link to the old Reading Company in its diamond-shaped logo, which is similar to that used by the railroad.

PRR's Suburban and 30th Street Stations

While the majority of large American railroad stations were completed by the mid-1920s, PRR continued to

This open-spandrel concrete arch bridge was built by the Pennsylvania Railroad over the Schuylkill River and Manayunk Canal at Manayunk as an improvement to its Schuylkill Valley line that ran northward to Reading, Pottsville, and New Boston. Much of the northern part of the line has been abandoned, and although this bridge once hosted SEPTA commuter trains, as of this writing in 2007, it lies unused. Sadly, while this railroad lies dormant, highway traffic on the nearby Schuylkill Expressway is near gridlock on most days. The tracks below the bridge along the canal are a former Reading Company industrial branch. The towpath of the old canal serves as bicycle path from Center City Philadelphia to Valley Forge. Brian Solomon

Philadelphia's western suburbs along the old Philadelphia & Columbia Railroad, later the Pennsylvania Railroad, are known as the Main Line—the name stemming from the old Main Line of Public Works. These communities were developed by the PRR as one of the first commuter suburbs. Today, the towns still benefit from regular SEPTA service. The town of Strafford has restored its Victorian-era railroad station that features classic gingerbread-style architecture.
Brian Solomon

invest in its Philadelphia terminals on a grand scale into the mid-1930s (when there was little major railroad investment anywhere). The railroad built the new downtown Suburban Station in 1930, after the old PRR Broad Street Station's immense train shed was destroyed in a catastrophic fire in 1923. The Broad Street Station's tracks reached the terminal over a controversial elevated structure known as the Chinese Wall, which separated the Market Street area west of city hall from districts north.

PRR's new Suburban Station, adjacent to the Broad Street Station, was better designed to serve commuters, had improved capacity, and ultimately simplified operations. The station's design was unusual at the time because its tracks and station facilities, as well as retail shops, were situated below street level. The space above served as commercial office space. Furthermore, the station had no grand waiting room. Instead, there was just an undistinguished mezzanine with a ticket counter over the tracks. Its above-ground entrance embodied a classic minimalist modern style—a total departure from Broad Street's intricate ornate Victorian styling. Today, Suburban Station's façade is regarded as a prime example of Art Deco style, although it wasn't designated Art Deco style during the time of its construction.

Designed by Philadelphia's Wilson Brothers and built by Charles McCall, Reading Terminal's vast balloon shed is the last surviving example of its type in the United States. Still common in England and across continental Europe, balloon sheds were once used at a number of large American terminal stations. The last train departed here on November 6, 1984. Spanning 253 feet, the shed's roof rises 95 feet above the old station platforms. When it was built, the shed was 509 feet long. Below, the old track-level Reading Terminal Market still thrives after more than 110 years. Brian Solomon

Suburban and Broad Street stations co-existed for more than 20 years. In April 1952, PRR closed and demolished its grand old Broad Street Terminal, which had been used for hourly long-distance trains from Center City to New York City, among other places. This shortsighted move was dismissed as progress at the time, despite the fact that the station had been among Philadelphia's finest structures.

In 1933, the Pennsylvania Railroad opened its impressive new station west of the Schuylkill River at 30th Street and Market in West Philadelphia. Designed by Alfred Shaw, this building blends a neo-classical Corinthian colonnade with contemporary Art Deco motifs. The station has tracks on two levels, the lower serving as Philadelphia's primary long-distance station and the upper handling suburban traffic en route to Suburban Station (and trains to Broad Street until 1952).

The station's main concourse is particularly impressive. Among the features is an enormous statue depicting an angel carrying a soldier skyward, symbolizing PRR's employees who perished in World War II. Along a wall near the washrooms is a huge relief mural rescued from Broad Street. It depicts the changes in transportation in the nineteenth century and even imagines the future of air transport as a dirigible-suspended steam engine hauling dirigible-suspended wooden railroad coaches.

Today, the 30th Street Station is Amtrak's primary Philadelphia station and is one of the busiest long-distance stations in the United States. Its Northeast Corridor trains to Boston, New York, and Washington; Keystone Corridor trains to Harrisburg; and long-distance trains to Pittsburgh, Florida, and places throughout the South all call here, making Philadelphia one of the best rail-served cities in the United States. After the closing of the Broad Street Station, eliminating direct Center City access for long-distance passengers, 30th Street passengers were allowed to ride free into Suburban Station from any upper-level train. SEPTA still honors that offer if you show an Amtrak ticket stub.

Above: SEPTA self-propelled electric multiple units working as the R7 local are seen against the Philadelphia skyline. SEPTA operates an intensive public transportation network using railroad lines of the old Pennsylvania Railroad and Reading Company, as well as the city's subways, trolleys, and buses.
Scott R. Snell

Left: The front of Reading Terminal faces one of Philadelphia's most important downtown thoroughfares—Market Street. Reading Terminal no longer serves as a railroad station. Instead SEPTA provides commuter service to Market Street East station, which is underground nearby. The grand days of entering Reading Terminal to board a train are gone, but at least the building survives. The same cannot be said for Pennsylvania Railroad's once-elegant Broad Street Station, demolished in an act of corporate vandalism in the 1950s.
Brian Solomon

CHAPTER 7

STRASBURG RAIL ROAD

By Kurt R. Bell

The Strasburg Rail Road Company of Lancaster County, Pennsylvania, traces its humble beginnings back to the railroad building fever of the 1830s. When the Philadelphia & Columbia Rail Road bypassed the town of Strasburg by some four miles, town residents decided they wanted the right to build their own short-line railroad to connect with the P&C. They knew that without a railroad connection, the town's economy would suffer irreparable damage. Their request for a railroad charter was granted by the Pennsylvania Legislature on June 9, 1832 (Bill No. 344).

The original 22 businessmen who invested in the railroad owned a total of 723 shares of stock. They hired Major Joshua Scott to survey the railroad from the home of Jacob Hoover (now the Swan Hotel) on the west end of Strasburg, down the center of the main street, and then east of town to connect with the P&C at or near Leaman's Place.

The bidding process to grade the entire line opened on December 11, 1834. Construction is believed to have begun the following year. But probably because of the economic panic of 1837, no tracks were laid. By the time the roadbed had been graded to within 100 yards of Leaman's Place—the junction point with the P&C just east of Paradise—promoters ran out of funds. The right-of-way languished for a decade before activity once again resumed.

By 1851, construction was in full swing again, and on February 12 of that year, the Strasburg Rail Road Company was incorporated. As part of the incorporation, more stock in the company was sold, which gave operators more capital to lay heavier rail and purchase a second-hand steam locomotive, the *William Penn*, from the P&C. Construction of the SRR was complete in late August, when the earliest train operations also began. By the end of that year, the railroad was interchanging freight cars at Leaman's

Facing page: One of the few railroads in Pennsylvania where steam locomotives operate a regular schedule on a daily basis is at Strasburg. During spring, summer, and fall, you can find locomotives on the move. Here, on an August evening, No. 90, a 2-10-0 Decapod, has just arrived from an excursion. This handsome locomotive was built by Baldwin in 1924 for the Great Western Railway in Loveland, Colorado. It has operated on the Strasburg Rail Road for more than 40 years and is a familiar sight puffing its way through the cornfields and glades on the run to Leaman's Place. Brian Solomon

Above: The sand dome on Strasburg No. 90 is a vital part of the locomotive. Sand is directed under the driving wheels to increase traction and prevent the wheels from slipping. This practice is especially important when starting a heavy freight train, but it can be useful in passenger operations as well. Skilled locomotive engineers will know by feel when sand is required, and they will control sand application from the cab. Brian Solomon

Place and running two round trips between Strasburg and Leaman's Place for those wanting to connect with passenger trains.

For several years, the line operated at a loss, and it was sold for $13,000 in a sheriff's sale in April 1859. The new owners were Feree Brinton and a group of 23 businessmen, including the honorable Thaddeus Stevens of Lancaster—the congressman who proposed the impeachment of President Andrew Jackson.

The operation continued until 1866, when John F. and Cyrus N. Herr purchased controlling interest. A. M. Herr later joined the company. In 1866, a large steam flour mill, planning mill, and machine shop were built at the Strasburg Terminal. Also within that same year, the company petitioned for a charter to extend the railroad to Quarryville to connect with the ore beds at Camargo. The effort was cut short by the financial panic of 1867. Four years later, a devastating fire destroyed the flour mill complex. The machine shop and planning mill were promptly rebuilt, but the Herrs had to sell the railroad by 1875.

The next owners, Thomas and Henry Baumgartner, bought the line for $12,725. Shortly thereafter, the Reading & Chesapeake RR proposed incorporating the SRR into its grand scheme of extending the line from Reading via Quarryville to the Chesapeake Bay region, but this dream died for unknown reasons. In 1888, Edward Musselman assumed operation of the railroad and continued to operate it for 10 years. In 1898, his relative Frank Musselman purchased the railroad and operated the line until 1918. Then State Senator John Homsher purchased the railroad and the feed mill. For the next 40 years, his sons, Fred L. and John J. Homsher and then a grandson, Bryon Homsher, operated the line. The principle commodities hauled were coal, lumber, grain, and feed.

Due in part to competition from the trucking industry and storm damage suffered from Hurricane Hazel in 1957, the SRR suspended freight operations and applied for abandonment with the ICC, which was never officially granted.

On November 1, 1958, Lancaster entrepreneur Henry Keiper Long, local plant engineer Donald Eugene Lindsey Hallock, and 23 businessmen and railroad

The Strasburg Rail Road operates one of the best maintained fleets of wooden-sheathed passenger cars that were typical of those found all across America in the early twentieth century. The old colloquial term "varnish," referring to named passenger trains, stems from the high gloss applied to wooden-sided cars. As all-steel cars became standard after 1910, the term slowly lost its meaning. However, railroaders continued to refer to varnish into the 1950s. Brian Solomon

Strasburg Rail Road trainman Kurt R. Bell checks his watch as locomotive No. 90 runs around the train. Using classic steam locomotives and vintage wooden-sheathed passenger cars, Strasburg recreates the golden age of railroad travel on its beautiful rural Pennsylvania branch line. Brian Solomon

The steam locomotive captures the spirit of traditional railroading, yet historic wooden-bodied freight cars are also key for recreating the period. Significantly smaller than their all-steel modern-day equivalents, these wooden cars display the names of companies such as Vermont's Rutland Railroad, which has long since vanished from the map. The Strasburg Rail Road recreates branch-line freights such as this one for photographers and enthusiasts who relish the sight of trains that ruled the landscape more than 70 years ago. Chris Bost

One of the gems sequestered among the steam locomotives at Strasburg is this General Electric 44-ton diesel, which was one of 45 built for the Pennsylvania Railroad. Restored to its traditional appearance, this locomotive was typical of those found on a variety of branches and industrial lines operated by the PRR in its last decades. Designed for tight curvature, this 44-ton switcher often towed boxcars through the streets in industrial districts of Philadelphia, working on factory sidings along the Main Line, or ambling through the countryside on light branches similar to Strasburg's tracks. Brian Solomon

Strasburg Rail Road No. 65 is a steel-frame wooden-body passenger coach built in 1910 by Harlan and Hollingsworth for the Reading Company. It was built during the transition from wooden- to steel-bodied cars. Notice the coal stove at the end of the car, which was used to heat the car on cold days, and the clerestory roof that was necessary to help ventilate it on hot days. "Air conditioning" was provided by opening the windows. Although it was used for ordinary travel, the car was designed with great details and styling. Brian Solomon

At the East Strasburg station, trainman Kurt R. Bell salutes a fellow member of the train crew prior to departure for Leaman's Place. Brian Solomon

buffs purchased the 50 outstanding shares of the railroad's stock from the Homsher estate for $18,000. The group rehabilitated the line on a hobby basis and began operating passenger excursions through the Pennsylvania Amish County on January 4, 1959.

On Labor Day weekend 1960, the railroad reintroduced steam power with ex-Canadian National 0-6-0 No. 31. From the 1960s to the beginning of the twenty-first century, the SRC grew into one of America's most successful steam tourist railroads. In its nearly 50 years of operation, it has hauled almost 14 million passengers. In 1998, the railroad began a thrice-annual tradition by hosting Day Out With Thomas™ events, which have introduced a whole new generation of youngsters to Thomas the Tank Engine and railroading heritage.

In addition to hauling a small number of freight cars, the company also derives its revenue from concession income, special events, and the contract repair work performed in its mechanical facilities. Clearly, in the context of railroading in Pennsylvania, the Strasburg is a modern business success story. As America's oldest surviving railroad that is still operating under its original charter, the line continues to prosper.

Editor's note: Kurt R. Bell is an archivist with the Pennsylvania Historical & Museum Commission at the Railroad Museum of Pennsylvania. As a conductor on the Strasburg RR since 1992, he has participated in the success of the company as both an employee and as a stockholder. His definitive book on the history of the Strasburg is forthcoming.

On the return run from Leaman's Place, Strasburg No. 90 approaches the Blackhorse Road crossing at Carpenters. The operating pressure on this locomotive is just under 200 pounds per square inch. When this capacity is exceeded, the safety valves lift and release excess steam from the boiler—an event that is evident in this image by the blast of steam exiting upward. Brian Solomon

The Strasburg Rail Road gives visitors the opportunity to observe and experience classic railroad cars and locomotives in action. These are more than just static museum pieces, but part of an active railroad. Locomotive No. 89 is a well-preserved example of an early twentieth-century Mogul-type locomotive. Its 2-6-0 wheel arrangement was well suited for light work on branch-line freight and passenger trains. It was built in 1910 by the Canadian Locomotive Company for the Grand Trunk Railway, a component of the Canadian National Railway that was formed in the 1920s. The locomotive has been entertaining Strasburg visitors since the 1970s. Brian Solomon

Western Maryland was a medium-sized railroad with main lines running from Baltimore to coal country around Elkins, West Virginia, and to Connellsville, Pennsylvania, for connections westward; other routes served Gettysburg and York, and ran from its hub at Hagerstown, Maryland, to Shippensburg, Pennsylvania. Largely a freight railroad, WM provided a nominal passenger service into the 1950s. This former WM parlor/smoking car was built in 1912 by Barney & Smith of Dayton, Ohio, at the end of the wooden car era. It has been working at the Strasburg Rail Road since 2005. Brian Solomon

This former Western Maryland parlor/smoking car serves Strasburg as the Warren F. Brenner *and is seen from the fireman's side of the boiler on locomotive No. 90 as it navigates the Strasburg yard at sunset.* Brian Solomon

Sunrise at Strasburg greets a new day. Soon droves of visitors will arrive to experience early twentieth-century railroading at its finest. Welcoming and enticing visitors is an atmosphere of classic railroading, including the historic J Tower, a Pennsylvania Railroad position light signal, and a selection of preserved locomotives and cars. Brian Solomon

Visiting Strasburg

It's rare in modern America to enter another age and behold the sight of a steam locomotive marching up the grade. Here, on the Strasburg Rail Road, this is a daily experience that invigorates the senses.

To take part in it, travel on Highway 896 south from Highway 30 and head south of the town of Strasburg. Then take Strasburg Road east toward Gap. Or you can drive the pastoral country roads and follow the smoke from the locomotive. The Strasburg Rail Road station is one and a half miles east of town (across the street from the Railroad Museum of Pennsylvania). If you decide to explore some of the area's pastoral country roads, you can always find your way back by following the smoke from the locomotive.

The Strasburg Rail Road is among the most charming and photogenic of the region's train rides. Its locomotives are well-maintained, highly polished operating gems of the steam age. Equally impressive is the railroad's fleet of immaculate wooden-bodied passenger cars that were once common in the early years of the twentieth century. Strasburg is one of a few excursion railroads to operate steam daily during its peak season (April through October).

Adding to the railroad's appeal are the traditional Amish and Mennonite communities that have made the area famous. The fields around the railroad are an oasis of rural charm in the ever-growing urban sprawl that is Lancaster.

The Strasburg Rail Road is preserved branch-line railroading at its best. The typical train ride departs the East Strasburg station at the top of the hour and takes about 45 minutes to make its ambling seven-mile round trip to Leaman's Place. Here, the railroad maintains a junction with the old main line of the Pennsylvania Railroad, now owned and operated by Amtrak. Passengers aboard the steam train may get a fleeting glimpse of Amtrak's Keystone Service trains—stainless-steel Amfleet passenger cars hauled by AEM-7 electrics or modern Genesis diesels—during their stop here. At Leaman's Place, Strasburg's steam locomotive runs around the train and gives passengers a chance to inspect the machinery as the locomotive saunters by and recouples to the other end of the train. For a first-class experience, pay the extra fare and ride on the parlor car. Not only can you ride in a more finely finished car and enjoy a beverage from the bar, but you will get a better view of the engine as it is coupled to the train.

Adjacent to the East Strasburg Station is the railroad's gift shop and bookstore. Inside, you will find one of the largest selections of railroad books anywhere in the commonwealth.

The pastoral scenery and rolling farms of Pennsylvania Dutch Country add to the rustic charm of the Strasburg Rail Road. Decapod No. 90 leads an excursion toward Strasburg from Leaman's Place on a hot, summer afternoon. This locomotive has resided on the Strasburg Rail Road since 1967.
Brian Solomon

CHAPTER 8

RAILROAD MUSEUM OF PENNSYLVANIA

The Railroad Museum of Pennsylvania, across the street from the historic Strasburg Rail Road Terminal, is one of the state's finest treasures. Its extensive collection of locomotives, rolling stock, artifacts, and archives reflects Pennsylvania's strong ties to railroading. Although other rail sites have significant and historic equipment, no other museum in Pennsylvania can boast of a more significant, well-organized, or relevant collection. "This is the *real* thing," said museum director David Dunn. "It's not a mockup or facsimile. There's value in the original."

Outside of the entrance to the museum, some of Pennsylvania's most famous locomotives beckon visitors. The museum's entrance is decorated with railroad heralds from the many different companies that have operated in the state over the years. Inside are even more treasures.

While the museum has many virtues, none is greater than the main hall where locomotives and railroad cars are displayed in a setting reminiscent

of a nineteenth-century passenger station train shed. A larger-than-life bronze statue of Alexander J. Cassatt—the Pennsylvania Railroad's visionary leader—presides over the collection. This is an exciting place filled with magnificent machines that exude the history of Pennsylvania's railroads. These great engines inspired so many children to delight in finding a train running around the tree on Christmas morning or beg to set up a model railroad in the basement.

PRR Collection

The Railroad Museum of Pennsylvania could easily be mistaken as a museum solely dedicated to featuring items from the Pennsylvania Railroad. No place on the planet has a more significant collection of PRR equipment.

In the golden age of railroading, PRR was the nation's largest railroad. It was integral in the development of Pennsylvania, as well as cities across the East and Midwest. Part of its legacy centers around

Facing page: Among the many restored locomotives in the Railroad Museum of Pennsylvania collection is former Pennsylvania Railroad 1223, a Class B16SB American type. Built by PRR's Juniata Shops in Altoona in 1905, this type of passenger locomotive was used on secondary trains and branch lines for many years. Old No. 1223 operated on the Strasburg Rail Road as late as 1989 before becoming a static display. Brian Solomon

Above: The Baldwin Locomotive Works was America's best known and most prolific producer of steam locomotives. Originally based in Philadelphia, the company later built a modern erection shop in the nearby suburb of Eddystone. By 1950, Baldwin had produced an estimated 59,000 steam locomotives and continued to build diesels into the mid-1950s. Virginia & Truckee Mogul-type No. 20 was built in Philadelphia in 1875. It is the oldest steam locomotive on display at the Railroad Museum of Pennsylvania. Brian Solomon

the development of many of the most significant, successful, and best-remembered twentieth-century steam locomotive designs. With the only substantive collection of PRR locomotives, the Railroad Museum of Pennsylvania can arguably boast the most significant modern collection in North America.

In the steam era, most American railroads ordered small batches of locomotives that were custom-designed based upon the empirical judgment of local motive power chiefs. By contrast, PRR systematically researched how to build better locomotives, applied scientific principles to those designs, and then built standardized machines with common interchangeable parts. Following a period of experimentation, PRR then ordered locomotives in large batches both from its own Juniata Shops in Altoona and from established builders, including Baldwin. PRR's oft-repeated slogan "Standard Railroad of the World" reflected its systematic standardized approach.

Thankfully, the PRR also had the foresight and resources to preserve its heritage by setting aside a collection that tells the story of twentieth-century locomotive development. Representative machines of most major locomotive types built between 1900 and 1930 were saved, most of which are proudly on display here today.

While going through the museum, make sure to compare PRR's machines such as the 4-4-2 Atlantic No. 7002—built with tall driving wheels for hauling passenger trains at speed—with the machines with smaller driving wheels designed for hauling heavy freight.

The Railroad Museum of Pennsylvania's main hall hosts the world's best preserved collection of Pennsylvania Railroad equipment. On the far left are examples of PRR's steam locomotives; Conrail GP30 2233 is an example of a 1960s-era diesel-electric, and PRR electrics GG1 4935 and E44 4465 are central to the exhibit. Not to be missed are examples of freight cars such as the Lehigh & New England coal hopper seen on the far right. Brian Solomon

Looking at these machines, you may wonder when steam ended on PRR, since all of the steam locomotives displayed here were built prior to 1930. Here lies an atypical tale of locomotive development. With the onset of the Great Depression and PRR's move toward large-scale electrification, the railroad had reduced its need for new steam power earlier than most railroads. Yet while it stopped placing large orders for new steam locomotives, it continued to experiment with steam locomotive technology. Based on this research, in the late 1930s and through the mid-1940s, PRR turned out some of the most impressive and unusual steam locomotives ever conceived. Sadly, these machines did not enjoy the commercial success of their older, tried-and-true cousins. PRR's peculiar high-speed T1 and heavy Q-class Duplex types were short-lived. They were withdrawn, while older engines continued to work in daily service. None of these oddities were preserved. Nor were PRR's massive J-class Texas types, built during World War II, or the one-of-a-kind experimental S-1 or the steam turbine S-2. These locomotives are represented by scale models in a glass case. Ultimately, the successful application of the diesel-electric spelled the end of steam. The end of PRR's steam operations finally came in 1957.

Alongside PRR's steam locomotives are a range of its straight electrics and diesel-electrics. PRR was among the pioneers of heavy railroad electrification in the early years of the twentieth century. On a visit to Paris in 1901, PRR President Alexander Cassatt was awed by the use of electricity for motive power at the Gare d'Orsay. Accordingly, PRR adopted an outside, electrified third rail for its Hudson River and East River tunnels that was built in conjunction with New York's Pennsylvania Station to emulate the French station arrangement. Later, PRR adopted overhead high-voltage alternating current electrification—first applying it to its Philadelphia suburban services and later extending this for main-line service on its busy New York–Philadelphia-Washington route, as well as for freight and passenger lines to Harrisburg. By 1939, PRR had the most extensive electrification in the world.

Outside of the museum is the last surviving example of PRR's third-rail, side-rod Class DD1 electric, built for service to New York's Pennsylvania Station. Adjacent is PRR's pioneering high-speed GG1 electric, No. 4800, known as "Old Rivets" for its riveted streamlined skin. Following extensive comparative testing, the GG1 design became PRR's choice for a standard high-

These beautifully restored and displayed Pennsylvania Railroad wooden-bodied passenger cars are typical of those used in the nineteenth century. Passenger trains typically carried mail and express cars, as well as baggage cars ahead of the passenger cars. PRR No. 6 pictured here was a typical baggage car of the period. It dates from 1882, and it was likely constructed in the railroad shops at Altoona. Express freight and mail shipments that moved on passenger trains were known as "head-end traffic" and contributed to the revenue from scheduled passenger trains, much in the way that freight moved in the belly of jet planes adds to airline revenue on long-haul flights today.
Brian Solomon

speed electric. Between 1935 and 1943, the railroad ordered 138 production GG1s.

However, before production began, PRR hired now-famous industrial designer Raymond Loewy to refine the GG1's image. Loewy suggested a welded skin, improved the appearance of external appendages, and designed the locomotive's famous paint scheme featuring a nearly black Brunswick green body and elegant gold cat's whiskers striping. Between the styling and the engineering, the GG1 was a hit and ruled the PRR electrified lines for more than four decades. They even outlasted the railroad by 15 years and made their final runs in 1983. During their heyday, PRR's GG1s raced between Philadelphia's 30th Street Station and Harrisburg and powered the railroad's luxury passenger trains, including the famous *Broadway Limited*. In their later years, they worked for both Amtrak and Conrail to haul freight and passenger trains.

Inside the main hall of the Railroad Museum of Pennsylvania is PRR GG1 Electric No. 4935. It was restored to its original livery by Amtrak in the late 1970s and repainted again in the 1980s. Today, it looks much the way Loewy intended. Among the other electrics displayed is the B1 boxcab that was used in later years as a switcher and a massive E44 freight electric built by General Electric at its locomotive works in Erie, Pennsylvania.

To some purists, the passing of the steam age represented the end of an era. Yet, diesels are an important part of the railroad story and are proudly featured at the museum. Several of PRR's historic diesels are here. The most significant is the last surviving Electro-Motive model E7, the best-selling passenger diesel of the postwar years.

The Electro-Motive Division of General Motors was the most successful of all diesel builders, and its E7 represented an evolutionary advance from the streamlined trains of the 1930s. It was bought by dozens of railroads around the country, and it rapidly displaced the Pacific, Hudson, and Northern-type steam locomotives from America's passenger trains. When PRR trials with this diesel demonstrated its exceptional cost efficiency and power, PRR gave up on its newest, most modern steam engines. The great T1 Duplex types, noted earlier, were sidelined as a result. While large numbers of later-model Es and similarly styled F-units have been preserved, this former PRR E7 is the only one to escape scrapping.

Diverse Displays

Other than an array of PRR equipment, the Railroad Museum of Pennsylvania has a number of other significant machines on display. Among them is a Baldwin-built 2-6-0 Mogul-type steam locomotive, the *Tahoe*, built in 1875 for Nevada's Virginia & Truckee. It represents the tens of thousands of locomotives built by the company, which was founded in Philadelphia by Matthias W. Baldwin in the 1830s. Over the years, Baldwin became synonymous with American-built steam power, and it sold locomotives to railroad companies across the United States and around the world. As the most prolific American steam builder, Baldwin produced an estimated 70,500 locomotives.

The museum also has equipment from many of the state's historic railroads, including the Reading Company, Western Maryland, Lehigh Valley, Maryland & Pennsylvania, and Lehigh & New England. Locomotives are just a portion of the display; there is also a superb selection of historic railroad cars, including the once-common ore-jenny—a variety of hopper used by the PRR to move iron ore to steel mills. You'll also see coal hoppers and a refrigerated boxcar or "reefer car"—used to keep fruit and vegetables chilled with large blocks of ice.

Passenger cars from several eras are here too, including Camden & Amboy No. 36. It was built in 1836 and is believed to be the second-oldest surviving

Developed for the Pennsylvania Railroad, the position light signal was one of the early railroad signals to use electric lamps. The signal's bright and focused yellow lights were visible in all types of ambient illumination, so signal aspects were unlikely to be confused with stray lights. This signal is displaying a "clear" aspect—meaning the track is free from obstruction. The signal is along the former Pennsylvania Railroad near Montgomery, Pennsylvania. Brian Solomon

passenger car in the United States. It is on loan from the Smithsonian Institution. Another passenger car worth checking out is Western Maryland business car No. 203, a classic heavyweight car built by Pullman in 1914 for railroad president Carl Gray. He asked that the car be sheathed with faux wooden siding to emulate the great business cars of the late nineteenth century. Also, all of the china, silver service, furniture, and furnishings are left in the car exactly as they were on its last day of service in 1969. Adjacent to the car is a map of the Western Maryland system showing its role as the central part of the Alphabet Route—a collective of several smaller railroads that moved east-west through freight in competition with the larger trunk lines. Today, little track remains on the old Western Maryland main line in Pennsylvania, as much of the line has been converted into a biking trail. A stretch of the WM's "Dutch" line is still intact from Gettysburg to York and is now operated by CSX; this is the same line over which Abraham Lincoln traveled to Gettysburg to give the Gettysburg Address.

At the back of the museum's exhibit hall is a display of railroad signals—those crucial pieces of hardware that kept the tracks safe and the lines fluid. Here, you'll find a rare example of an early automatic block signal, known as a Hall disc signal, used on the Reading Company's Newtown branch at Huntington Valley, Pennsylvania. These are often described by railroaders as a banjo signal because of their distinctive shape that resembles the body of the bluegrass musical instrument. Invented by Thomas Seavey Hall in 1869, the signal was first mass-produced in 1871. Some railroads, including the Reading Company, continued to use Hall disc signals through the 1940s.

Position light signals that were used by the Pennsylvania Railroad and Baltimore & Ohio are also here. Visitors may set the aspects on the PRR signal, which uses an arrangement of lights to mimic the common semaphore positions. On modern railroads, semaphores and position-light signals have been largely replaced with electric color-light hardware that display red, yellow, green, and sometimes white light to govern train movements.

Throughout the museum are samples of railroad art and artifacts that help visitors learn the technology, business, and glory of railroading. In the administrative offices above the museum is one of the best archives of railroad literature and images, which are available to researchers by appointment.

The Railroad Museum of Pennsylvania offers an excellent display of classic freight and passenger cars. This demonstration portrays how a refrigerated boxcar was re-iced in the days before mechanical refrigeration. Fruit Growers Express 57708, built in 1924, was used to move citrus products from Florida to markets in the Northeast. Long trains of refrigerated cars operated on expedited schedules with pre-planned icing stops en route. Today, fruit is moved by rail in much larger cars with mechanical refrigeration and more commonly transported in refrigerated highway trailers on piggyback trains. Brian Solomon

CHAPTER 9

TAKE A RIDE ON THE READING

Although the biggest and best known in the region, the Strasburg Rail Road and Railroad Museum of Pennsylvania have no monopoly on historic railroading. Several branches of the former Reading Company were developed as short-line tourist railroads in the 1960s and 1970s and continue to attract and entertain visitors.

Wanamaker, Kempton & Southern

Nestled along Ontelaunee Creek and in sight of the ridgeline formed by the Blue Mountain—one of numerous natural diagonals that both divide and define Pennsylvania—is one of Pennsylvania's most charming and obscure tourist railways. The Wanamaker, Kempton & Southern in Kempton operates on a classic, rural Pennsylvania branch line in an environment uncluttered by suburban sprawl and modern development. Unlike many excursion railroads that are operating today, WK&S's line was never more than a rural country branch, which is evidenced in the character of the line.

The line was conceived during the great railroad building boom that followed the American Civil War. It was chartered in 1870 as the Berks County Railroad. The line that survives today was originally part of a scheme to connect anthracite coal fields with industries in the Reading area in order to compete with the Philadelphia & Reading. It was completed in 1874. At that time, it extended northeast just over 43 miles from Cumru Junction south of Reading to a connection with the Lehigh Valley at Little Run Junction. Unfortunately, the flood of anthracite from Lehigh Valley never materialized. By the end of 1874, the Berks County Railroad was reorganized and leased to the Philadelphia & Reading (Reading Company after 1893). For about a century, it was run as Reading's Schuylkill & Reading branch.

With the tide of coal flowing over other routes and little through traffic, the branch had a relatively quiet existence serving local communities.

Facing page: The Lehigh & New England four-wheel wooden caboose No. 572 spent most of its career on the back of local freights and coal runs in eastern Pennsylvania. By the time it was retired, it was a twentieth-century operating anomaly, as the vast majority of railroad freight equipment now rides on pairs of four-wheel trucks. Yet, in the early days of American railroading, four-wheel cars were typical. This historic caboose is preserved along with other L&NE cars on the WK&S at Kempton. Brian Solomon

Above: Middletown & Hummelstown No. 91, a 2-6-0 Mogul type built in the early years of the twentieth century, is a popular attraction today. Brian Solomon

Ultimately, it was this lack of traffic that gave the line its charm. This route had little need for substantial upgrading or modernization. In fact, the Schuylkill & Reading branch always featured relatively light rails with wooden ties on cinder ballast and a sinuous path.

In its heyday, the line hosted a pair of daily passenger trains and freight. In 1881, morning branch passengers departed Reading at 8:20 a.m. They traveled the one hour and 28 minutes over 24 miles to Kempton and stopped at numerous small stations along the way. Freight trains on the line were generally short and consisted of perhaps 10 to 12 cars of various types that were intended for local delivery. In the nineteenth century, 4-4-0 American-type locomotives hauled the trains. Some were the unusual Camelback variety—anthracite burners with a huge firebox that resulted in two cabs: one straddling the boiler for the engineer and another at the back for the fireman. In later steam days, Reading Company's bituminous-burning 2-8-0s were typically used.

As with many lightly used branches, the decline of this line began as local highways were improved.

Passenger service was curtailed in 1949; after that, Reading began trimming the line. In 1962, the line was cut north (east) of Kempton.

The abandonment of regular freight services beyond Kempton presented an opportunity for the creation of a tourist railway on an unused portion of the line. Enough time had passed since the elimination of steam locomotives on American main lines for the public to develop nostalgia for historic railway operations. By the early 1960s, enthusiasm for steam excursions was riding a wave in eastern Pennsylvania, and the founding of Strasburg Rail Road as a tourist line, as well as Reading Company's own Reading Ramble excursions, had created a market for nostalgic railway trips. In 1963, the Wanamaker, Kempton & Southern initiated excursions on a three-and-one-half-mile section of the old Schuylkill & Reading branch.

Initially, the railroad was still connected to the American railroad network with an interchange at Kempton with the Reading Company. Service on this end of the branch became increasingly infrequent by

Built in November 1925 for South Carolina's Lancaster & Chester Railroad, old No. 40 has been a star attraction on the New Hope & Ivyland excursion train for many years. A mid-day departure finds No. 40 storming out of town, with its whistle howling and bell ringing. New Hope's classic passenger station can be seen to the right of the train. Brian Solomon

the late 1960s. In the early 1970s, Reading abandoned the line north of Evansville and sold most of it for scrap, although WK&S acquired another mile to the village of North Albany.

Visiting the Hawk Mountain Line

Although less well known than the Strasburg Rail Road, the Wanamaker, Kempton & Southern shares many of the same attractions for the avid train rider. The easy pace of operation and picturesque rural scenery make for a relaxing day on the railroad.

Train rides are offered most weekends from May through October. Riders are treated to vintage passenger cars that are hauled by either steam or light diesel locomotives. Among WK&S's passenger cars are three former Reading Company all-steel cars that are similar to those used on the line when it stopped scheduled passenger services. Two of the cars are day coaches that were constructed for the Reading Company by The Harlan & Hollingsworth Corporation of Wilmington, Delaware, between 1913 and 1916. These are among the earliest all-steel coach designs that were built during the transitional period from wooden-bodied equipment. Another car is a combine (coach/baggage car) built in 1923. The railroad also has a Delaware, Lackawanna & Western all-steel day coach that features the common clerestory roof that was characteristic of cars used on branch lines in the latter steam era.

Among the freight cars on the line are several historic pieces from the Lehigh & New England Railroad, including an anthracite hauler that once operated a route to the far side of Blue Mountain. WK&S often operates freight cars and cabooses together with passenger cars to give passengers a choice of riding experiences.

The atmosphere around the Kempton station recreates the feeling of a typical, small-town branch. Although the original Kempton station was located in the center of town—somewhat south of the present location—today's station building is an authentic Reading Company depot. According to the railroad's brochure, *A Passenger's Guide to the Train Ride from Kempton to Wanamaker*, the station building was moved to Kempton from nearby Joanna, Pennsylvania, on the old Wilmington & Northern branch. In addition to the main track, there are several additional tracks used for running the locomotive around the train and for car storage.

Standing tall across from the ticket window is a classic train order signal. It was used in the days of

Once common, the steam locomotive was the staple form of transportation for more than 100 years. Old No. 40 was built in 1925, which was the same year the first commercial successful diesel-electric locomotive was built. Brian Solomon

The interior of New Hope & Ivyland's first-class passenger car displays the type of accommodation typical for the railroad's 45-minute round trip from New Hope to Lahaska. Brian Solomon

Re-lettered for the Lancaster & Chester Railroad, the road the locomotive was built for, New Hope & Ivyland 2-8-0 No. 40 leads a charter freight train at Buckingham Valley, Pennsylvania. This handsome locomotive is characteristic of those built by Baldwin in Philadelphia for freight service during the first two decades of the twentieth century. Chris Bost

timetable and train order operation to alert train crews that a stop for orders was required. Orders would have been transmitted by telegraph (or by telephone in later years), translated onto paper by the operator, and used to amend the timetable and provide operating instructions and authorization to train crews. Farther down the yard is an electrically operated semaphore, the type used by operators in manual block territory to govern train movements. Although WK&S does not use these signals in day-to-day operations, they lend to the historical atmosphere around the station.

While off-the-beaten path, the WK&S is not hard to find. It is just five to six miles north of Interstate 78 and about 25 minutes east of Allentown. Visitors from the east should take Route 737 north to Kempton, while visitors from the west may take Route 143, both of which are served by exits off Interstate 78.

New Hope & Ivyland

The historic village of New Hope, along the Delaware River, is about an hour's drive northeast of Philadelphia.

Situated on the old Delaware division of the Pennsylvania Canal, the town is famous for its quaint Victorian architecture and antique shops. The terminus of the New Hope & Ivyland is located off West Bridge Street, a couple of blocks west of North Main Street. In the mid-1960s, the New Hope & Ivyland began running steam excursions on a branch acquired from the Reading Company. Today, the New Hope & Ivyland operates this meandering 17-mile-long branch line that connects its namesake towns. In addition to hosting excursions between New Hope and the rural halt at Lahaska Station, the railroad provides freight service.

The rail station in New Hope is very quaint; it's an 1891 Victorian gingerbread building that has been beautifully restored. In *Great American Railroad Stations*, author Janet Greenstein Potter notes that the station was saved from demolition in the 1950s, moved away from the tracks, and used as a clubhouse. A decade later, it was relocated trackside again, near its old location. Today, it serves as NH&I's ticket office and retains the charm of a classic, small-town railroad station.

In November 1975, New Hope & Ivyland No. 40 was unmistakably a tourist steam locomotive with its white-wall tires, safety-yellow grab irons, and sans-serif lettering on the tender. For the better part of four decades, this old Baldwin has been entertaining visitors and allowing children to experience a real live steam locomotive—all while keeping part of the old Reading Company alive.
George W. Kowanski

In season, NH&I typically operates three trains daily with as many as eight trips during special events. Most excursions are under an hour long, and trains may be boarded at either station. While the New Hope station is easier for most visitors to reach and has more attractions, it charges a nominal fee for parking.

As of 2007, most trains departing here are hauled by diesels. On some weekends and special occasions, NH&I's No. 40, a 1925-built Baldwin 2-8-0 Consoli-dation-type

steam locomotive, is the star attraction. Built as South Carolina's Lancaster & Chester Railway No. 40, the engine has resided at New Hope since 1966. The railroad also has two additional steam locomotives, which at the time of this book's publication were awaiting restoration. The railroad's passenger cars are classic all-steel heavyweights. Both first- and second-class seating is available; the primary benefit of first class is that its seats are in a climate-controlled car with bar service.

With the rise of the automobile, branch line railroads were the first to suffer. From the 1920s onward, many branches were cut back or abandoned altogether. The culture of the rural line, with its stations and friendly agents, faded during the mid-twentieth century. Too many lines were closed, leaving only a broken right-of-way, photos, memories, and, on frosty autumn evenings, the passing of the occasional ghost train. Brian Solomon

Most rural lines, as well as many secondary main lines, were traditionally operated using specific rules known as "timetable and train orders." The company timetable authorized train movements by time, class, and direction. Amendments to the timetable—necessitated by late-running trains, extra sections, or extra trains—were accommodated with train orders. These orders were issued from a central dispatching office by telegraph to line side telegraph operators—often working in stations or signal towers—who would then deliver orders to passing trains. This train order signal at Kempton, Pennsylvania, indicates green lights in both directions which means that there are no orders. If one of the arms was in the stop position, trains traveling in that direction would be compelled to stop and collect orders. Brian Solomon

The caboose was the domain of a freight train's conductor. He rode at the back of the train and was charged with the details of operation. The conductor, rather than the locomotive engineer, was actually in charge of the train. It was his job to ensure it ran in accordance with the rules of the railroad and arrived safely and on time. Many cabooses, such as this one built for the Reading Company, had tall cupolas to give the conductor or a rear-end brakeman a perch in which to sit and watch for problems with the train as it rolled along. Among the most common problem was the dreaded "hotbox," caused by an overheated wheel journal. This could often be spotted by the telltale sign of bluish-white smoke emanating from the journal, accompanied by an acrid odor. Brian Solomon

Traditionally, switch lanterns were used on the top of switch stands to indicate the direction of the switch. In this case, a green light indicates the switch is "normal," meaning it's set for the main route; a red light indicates the switch is "reversed" and set for the diverging route. Inside the lantern, an oil lamp burns, and the switch lantern lenses were designed to magnify the light of the flame so that it might be better seen at a distance. In large yards, railroads employed a whole craft of men to maintain the lanterns and ensure the lamps were filled with oil. Brian Solomon

Few railroads encapsulate the charm of a rural branch line as successfully as the Wanamaker, Kempton & Southern. Built to haul coal, the line survived for most of its commercial existence as a backwater on the old Reading Company system. For more than 40 years, it has been entertaining visitors as a classic train ride. On an August afternoon, WK&S No. 65 works upgrade from Wanamaker on its return run to Kempton. Brian Solomon

Middletown & Hummelstown

The Middletown & Hummelstown Railroad is a modern short line that connects the nearby towns that comprise its name. According to a November 1989 article by Ronald S. Martin and Wendell J. Dillenger in *Railpace*, the original M&H was a 6.5-mile-long line chartered in 1888, and it operated from the time of its completion in 1890 until 1976 as the Middletown branch of the Reading Company. The line connected with Reading's main line to Harrisburg at Hummelstown and maintained an interchange with PRR's main line at Middletown.

The builder's plate on Wanamaker, Kempton & Southern No. 65. The H. K. Porter Company of Pittsburgh specialized in a stock catalog of small- to moderate-sized industrial locomotives. It built an estimated 8,200 locomotives between 1866 and 1950. Brian Solomon

Early twentieth-century grade crossing protection did little more than admonish users of the highways to watch out for trains. The legal burden was on the motorist, pedestrian, or carriage driver to avoid getting struck by the train. In those days, it was hard to miss the sight of an approaching locomotive. Therefore, a heavy cast-iron sign was deemed sufficient crossing protection. Wanamaker, Kempton & Southern No. 65 works the yard in Kempton on a September evening. Brian Solomon

Traditional scheduled passenger service through here appears to have ended in 1939. After Hurricane Agnes damaged the line in 1972, the Reading Company ended freight service on the branch. The present M&H short line started on the eve of Conrail in 1976. It began operating as a tourist railway in 1986.

Visiting the M&H

Today, the railroad styles itself as the Milk & Honey Line. It operates both as a carrier freight service to

shippers along its line and a popular weekend passenger excursion. The primary freight interchange is with Norfolk Southern at Middletown, which requires the railroad to run on a fascinating section of street trackage for several blocks in the center of town.

Street trackage, which once was remarkably common, only remains in a few Pennsylvania cities. To avoid accidents, M&H freights travel at restricted speeds down the street while the conductor walks ahead of the train with a red flag to warn motorists and pedestrians of

Above: *Middletown & Hummelstown No. 91 was built in the early years of the twentieth century. Today, it's a popular attraction on this short line and tourist railroad that operates just a few miles east of Harrisburg.* Brian Solomon

Facing page, upper left: *Built for the Safe Harbor Water Power Corporation in 1930, locomotive No. 65 was used in construction of the Safe Harbor Dam along the Susquehanna River. Since its acquisition by the Wanamaker, Kempton & Southern in 1970, No. 65 has been a popular attraction. It's a handsome saddle-tank type with a 0-6-0T wheel arrangement, and it is typical of small switch engines used all across the United States.* Brian Solomon

Facing page, upper right: *Wanamaker, Kempton & Southern crew members discuss logistics at the ticket window of the Kempton, Pennsylvania, station on a warm September evening. Some 80,000 stations once dotted North America, and virtually every town of importance had at least one. Railroad stations were lively places and the center of local activity. In addition to servicing the needs of passengers and small freight shippers, many railroad stations also served as operations centers where a telegraph operator would receive orders from train dispatchers. This station has the telegraph code of KN.* Brian Solomon

Facing page, bottom: *Wanamaker, Kempton & Southern No. 65 is under steam at the Kempton station after finishing its Harvest Moon special run to Wanamaker and back. Evening runs are a special treat. Away from the hustle and bustle of urban life, the WK&S rural steam-powered night trains allow passengers and passersby to experience all the sounds and smells of traditional railroading, magnified by the darkness. The mournful whistle in the distance conjures up images of a simpler, easier time.* Brian Solomon

With a hiss of steam, Middletown & Hummelstown No. 91 eases forward from the engine shed and shop at Middletown. Quiet for nearly three years while it was being overhauled, this old Canadian National Mogul is again alive. The Mogul was among the more popular types in the nineteenth century. Locomotive historian Alfred Bruce noted that the type was built in the United States continuously from 1860 to 1910. The first 2-6-0s seemed enormous and vastly more powerful compared with the early locomotives of the pre-Civil War period, thus their name Mogul, which implied great power. Brian Solomon

the train's approach. This is in stark contrast to the now-removed former Nickel Plate Road street trackage on 19th Street in Erie, Pennsylvania, where main line Norfolk Southern freights, often a mile long, would roll down the street at a steady 15 to 20 miles per hour at least eight times a day. The M&H freights that run to Middletown are normally hauled by one of two vintage Alco diesel-electric switchers.

M&H's passenger excursions depart from its restored brick freight station at Middletown. They typically make a 10-mile round trip along M&H's main line near the old Union Canal towpath along Swatara Creek. Excursions generally do not operate on the street trackage, nor is the trackage to the NS interchange at Hummelstown in regular service. Passengers travel in vintage 1920s-era Delaware, Lackawanna & Western suburban passenger cars. Depending on availability of motive power, these may be hauled by a vintage General Electric center-cab switcher or M&H's former Canadian National 2-6-0 Mogul-type steam locomotive. This steam locomotive was built in 1910 by the Canadian Locomotive Company and has worked the M&H since 1988.

M&H's station is just a short walk from Amtrak's Middletown Station, which is served by daily electric Keystone Corridor trains between Philadelphia's 30th Street Station and Harrisburg. Since schedules of both railroads vary, it's best to check ahead of time before embarking on an all-rail excursion.

Over the years, M&H has collected a variety of historic railroad equipment. Most of the equipment is stored near its Middletown Station. It has a variety of old trolley cars, as well as several freight and passenger cars. Among the most interesting cars is an old wooden boxcar that dates from the time of link and pin couplers.

Middletown & Hummelstown operates a former Reading Company branch between its namesake towns. In addition to hosting popular excursions, M&H provides a weekday freight service to customers in the Middletown area. On its way to interchange with Norfolk Southern in Middletown, this short M&H local freight led by Alco S6 switcher 151 negotiates several blocks of street trackage. To protect the train, the conductor walks ahead of the locomotive with a red flag. Once common in many cities, railroad street trackage is now rare in Pennsylvania. Brian Solomon

On its first public trip following a major overhaul, Middletown & Hummelstown No. 91 leads an excursion across the tall plate girder bridge over Swatara Creek on September 29, 2007. This former Canadian National 2-6-0 Mogul is similar to No. 89 operated by the Strasburg Rail Road. Brian Solomon

PART III

THROUGH THE MOUNTAINS VIA THE HORSESHOE CURVE

The anthracite lines in eastern Pennsylvania were conceived as conveyors of coal, but the Main Line, as it was known, was envisioned as a gateway to the West. Initially sponsored by the commonwealth, the corridor established by the Main Line was eventually dominated by the Pennsylvania Railroad. Although it has evolved over the years, changed ownership several times, and is no longer the primary avenue for westward passenger transport that it was in the nineteenth century, the old Main Line remains a heavy artery for freight transport. It is among the busiest freight railroads in the eastern United States.

Today, this route offers visitors the opportunity to explore its unique heritage, while enjoying the passage of heavy freight trains in a mountainous environment. In addition to sites and museums such as the Allegheny Portage Railroad and the Altoona Railroaders Museum, a number of towns on the west slope of the mountain cater to railroad enthusiasts. They have even built train-watching areas to encourage railroad tourism.

Johnstown offers a variety of interesting historical railroad vantage points. Famous for its 1889 flood, when a wall of water inundated the city, Johnstown has been an important point on the route between Pittsburgh and Philadelphia since the days of the Main Line of Public Works. PRR's old stone arch bridge at this location acted as a dam that held back tons of debris that later caught fire in the 1889 flood. On a fine November morning, a westward Norfolk Southern train glides across the Conemaugh River, which has been channelized. A park at the confluence of the Conemaugh and Stonycreek offers a pleasant place to watch the railroad roll. Brian Solomon

CHAPTER 10

Main Line of Public Works

Since its formative days, America has set its sight westward. From 1817 through 1825, the newest way west was through the Erie Canal. It was an important transport link with the Great Lakes that avoided the treacherous obstacle of Niagara Falls. The canal was an immediate success, and with it New York City flourished from traffic moving to and from the rapidly growing Midwest. The canal's importance set an example for entrepreneurs, politicians, and transport visionaries who attempted to emulate its success again and again.

Until the Erie Canal snatched away the lion's share of interior traffic, Pennsylvania served as a conduit for traffic moving to the Midwest. Some of it followed the natural waterways of the Delaware and Susquehanna rivers, and then it moved over the mountains. As a result, Pittsburgh had grown as an inland port because of its strategic location where the Allegheny and Monongahela rivers form the Ohio. Together, the Ohio and Mississippi provided a natural navigable waterway all the way to New Orleans and the Gulf of Mexico. In those days, a trip between Philadelphia and Pittsburgh took between 18 and 35 days, depending on weather; in winter, travel was virtually impossible.

Once the Erie Canal was completed, officials in Pennsylvania were anxious to forge a better way to transport goods across the state. Yet, the state's natural obstacles proved difficult to negotiate. Where New York was blessed with the Mohawk River Valley's natural gap in the Appalachian range, Pennsylvania faced crossing the spine of the mountains. To overcome this impediment, the commonwealth sponsored the Main Line of Public Works in 1826. This odd system blended a variety of transport modes to connect Philadelphia and Pittsburgh.

Facing page: Often credited as the first railroad tunnel in the United States, the 901-foot-long Staple Bend Tunnel is located about four miles from Johnstown. It may be reached by driving to a parking area near Mineral Point and walking about 2.5 miles of the old Allegheny Portage Railroad right-of-way maintained by the National Park Service. This September afternoon view shows the ornate classic relief that adorns the west portal. It was one of the most expensive engineering projects of the Portage Railroad. Brian Solomon

Above: At the top of plane No. 6, a number of re-created elements of the Allegheny Portage Railroad are open for public inspection. Since very little of the old railroad survived, it has been necessary to rebuild portions of the line. For example, this section of strap-iron track and the replica engine house give visitors a sense for what the railroad was like during its day. Inside, the building is a full-scale model of the old stationary engine used to haul canal boats and rail cars with hemp ropes. Brian Solomon

A detailed plan for the Main Line was unveiled in 1828, years of discussion ensued, and construction finally began in 1831.

The first section of the Main Line of Public Works was building the Philadelphia & Columbia Rail Road, a largely a grade-level railroad between its namesake points. The two steep gradients on this line were traversed with inclined planes and stationary engines. The famous Belmont Plane was located just west of downtown Philadelphia in the area now occupied by Fairmont Park. The other inclined plane was near Columbia, where the railroad met the canal that represented the next stage of the Main Line. This canal followed a natural waterway of the Susquehanna and Juniata rivers to Hollidaysburg—a settlement near the foot of the Allegheny Divide. Surmounting these mountains was the famed Allegheny Portage Railroad (described in detail below) between Hollidaysburg and Johnstown, with the remainder of the journey to Pittsburgh completed by canal.

RELIANCE TRANSPORTATION COMPANY.
(VIA)
Pennsylvania Rail Roads and Canals
FROM PHILADELPHIA TO PITTSBURG

By means of Transhipping IRON CANAL BOATS, in which Goods are placed at Philadelphia and pass together with the Boats to Pittsburg with Safe certainty and unprecedented despatch. Emigrants and others travelling with their effects can be accommodated with a cheap & expediti passage West.

Agents: JAMES M. DAVIS   Pittsburg.
Jno DOUGHERTY   Philadelphia.
McKEE & LOUDEN   New York.

Freight-forwarding agent John Dougherty of Philadelphia was the man behind Reliance Transportation Company. In 1834, he developed a popular variety of sectional canal packet used on the Main Line of Public Works and shipped over the Allegheny Portage Railroad. This period advertisement provides a sense of how the canal and railroad looked and how boats were transferred from the canal to railroad cars. Notice the primitive locomotives used to haul cars over the level sections of the Portage Railroad. W. A. Lucas collection, Railroad Museum of Pennsylvania PHMC

The Work's canals opened by 1832, and the Portage Railroad was open two years later. Although each of the components of the Main Line was based on an established means of transport, nothing like the Main Line had ever been built as a unified corridor. The awkward and complex nature of the Main Line's component systems made for something less than an efficient means of transport. The railroad portion between Philadelphia and Columbia functioned more like a turnpike of the era—an improved toll road. It was lightly and crudely built and essentially open to anyone who wished to transport wagons over it for a fee.

Possessing neither the beauty and simplicity of a canal, nor the unity and speed of a proper steam railway, the Main Line was a commercial flop. It was like a state-run Zeppelin in a world of private jet planes. By the time the Main Line was in operation, the steam railroad had come into its own and numerous railroads were in operation or under construction. Although inadequate, the Main Line established a transportation corridor through Pennsylvania that remains active and vital today.

Allegheny Portage Railroad

The most distinctive, most interesting, and best remembered portion of the Main Line was the 36.9-mile-long fairytale-like Allegheny Portage Railroad. This line used a series of inclined plancs to haul canal packets over the spine of the Alleghenies. It was inspired by the success of the Delaware & Hudson's coal-hauling railroad.

The line utilized five inclined planes on either side of the divide—each double track—with conventional

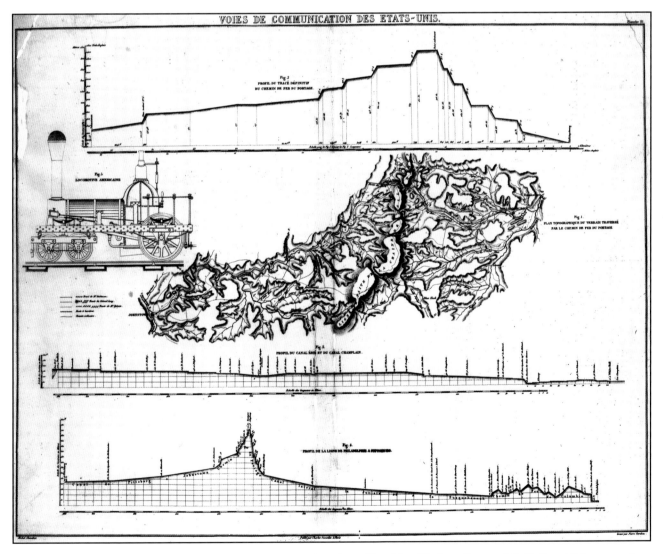

This period document, written in French, provides a map and grade profile of the Allegheny Portage RR. Railroad Museum of Pennsylvania PHMC

level sections in between the inclines. The longest level was located near Johnstown on the west slope and covered just over 13 miles. The most significant feature of the west slope was the 901-foot-long Staple Bend Tunnel that is four miles east of Johnstown—often credited as the first railway tunnel in the United States. Where conventional railway lines rarely use ascending gradients steeper than 2 percent (a rise of two feet per every hundred traveled), these inclined planes ascended grades of 8 percent to 10 percent. Canal packets and rail cars moved in sections on the inclined planes and were attached to cables with clamps.

Moving westward, the five planes on the east slope of the Alleghenies ascended roughly 1,400 feet (more than a quarter mile) to the summit at Blairs Gap—2,232 feet above sea level. To travelers on the Portage Railroad, getting to this wild mountain summit in a canal packet must have seemed like reaching the top of

the world—a virtual sea of trees spread out below as far as the eye could see. Descending to Johnstown and the waters of the Little Conemaugh River required less of a steep drop, although the western terminus of the line was still 1,175 feet lower than the summit.

The system that required the canal packets to be hoisted out of the water and slowly moved up the inclined planes seemed extremely slow, but it was generally faster than transloading the contents of the packets to railroad wagons for shipment over the mountain (although both methods were used). According to *Centennial History of the Pennsylvania Railroad*, hauling shipments over the line took about four hours. Other sources indicate that it was closer to six hours.

The Pennsylvania Railroad briefly used the line between 1852 and 1854, while its engineers were working on the construction of an all-rail route over the mountains. In that brief transitional time, the Main

CROSSING OF THE ALLEGHANY, PENNSYLVANIA RAILROAD.

This lithograph from about 1852 is an artist's impression of the Portage Railroad. It shows several successive inclined planes and a locomotive-powered train on a level section. Moncure Robinson, who engineered the Portage Railroad, went on to build the Philadelphia & Reading. W. A. Lucas collection, Railroad Museum of Pennsylvania PHMC

Near the base of plane No. 6 is this old skewed masonry arch that carried a road across the Portage Railroad. The alignment of the plane is evident on the right. At the top of the plane is the replica of the engine house. Visitors to the Allegheny Portage Railroad Site may walk along the old plane to reach the bridge, which sits between east and westward lanes of old Highway 22. Brian Solomon

Line was still working, but so were the steam-hauled trains of the PRR. Both relied on the cable-hauled inclined planes to move their traffic over the mountains.

Visiting the Allegheny Portage Railroad Site

While it lasted for only a generation, the Portage Railroad has held a fascination for Americans since the nineteenth century. Today, one of Pennsylvania's most unusual railroad preservation sites is the Allegheny Portage Railroad National Historic Site, which is run by the National Park Service. Although legislation preserving the site dates back to August 1964, the park as it exists today is more recent and has two primary sites along the line of the long-defunct Portage Railroad.

The first is a museum with a well-designed interpretive visitor's center that was built in 1992. It is just several miles from Horseshoe Curve and close to popular railroad sites at Gallitzin and Cresson. Located at the top of Blairs Gap Run, just off Highway 22, this museum is the site of the old Portage Railroad's Summit Level and its Incline No. 6—the highest of five inclines on the east slope of the mountain. Open year-round, this staffed facility features restrooms, an information desk, and a small theater where a short film about the railroad is presented. Among the highlights

here are a working-scale model of an inclined plane, sections of rebuilt tracks, and a replica of the building that housed stationary steam engines used to operate Incline No. 6.

Nearby is the famous Lemon House, an inn once used by travelers on the Main Line. Down toward the foot of Incline No. 6 is a skewed stone arch bridge that sits between the east and westbound lanes of old Highway 22. It is a brisk walk downhill to the top of the plane and a hardy climb back.

The second official Portage Railroad site, the Staple Bend Tunnel, is located near Mineral Point, about four miles east of Johnstown. Although it has long been listed on regional topographic maps, this tunnel only opened to the public in 2001. Along the old right-of-way are remnants of the Portage Railroad, including some of the old stone sleepers used to hold the rails in place, as well as abutments and stone culverts. Much of the line is parallel to Norfolk Southern's former Pennsylvania Railroad main line, which can be seen at various locations through the trees. Walking through the 901-foot-long tunnel takes you into the inky gloom of the mountain with only the light at the other end and a railing to serve as a guide. Less bold adventurers are advised to carry a flashlight.

CHAPTER 11

THE PENNSYLVANIA RAILROAD AND THE HORSESHOE CURVE

After a decade of operation, the inherent inadequacies of the Main Line of Public Works were well known. It had not carried the volume of traffic needed to put Philadelphia back on par with New York, and the system was unprofitable. By the 1840s, a number of railroads had been built in mountainous terrain and demonstrated that an ordinary railroad could be built across the Alleghenies. Pennsylvania officials decided that adding a privately operated steam railroad to Pittsburgh was necessary.

The Baltimore & Ohio, chartered to connect the port of Baltimore with the Ohio River, already had been planning an extension to Pittsburgh at the time. However, it would divert traffic through Baltimore, not Philadelphia. In April 1846, Pennsylvania's governor signed legislation that authorized both the construction of the Pennsylvania Railroad to Pittsburgh and the B&O extension, although the latter provision was phrased to exclude the B&O if the PRR got organized first.

Since the state-run Philadelphia & Columbia already reached the Susquehanna, and another railway called the Harrisburg, Portsmouth, Mount Joy & Lancaster connected the P&C with Harrisburg, PRR's original charter specified it could build west to Pittsburgh from a connection with the HPMtJ&L at Harrisburg.

In 1847, PRR made a wise selection in hiring chief engineer J. Edgar Thomson to survey the line. Thomson was one of the most experienced railroad men of his day, and he learned his trade on the ground. Thomson had spent fifteen years building and operating railways. Among other railroads, he worked for Camden & Amboy and Philadelphia & Columbia—lines later integrated into the PRR system under his leadership. His success as an engineer served him well, and Thomson rose to become PRR's third president. In that role, he set standards for knowledgeable leadership that remained with the company for generations.

Facing page: In 1992, a new Horseshoe Curve visitor's center opened. This center included a modern funicular railroad to bring passengers to the top. Painted like PRR passenger diesels of the postwar period, the funicular makes for a nice ride. It is easier on the feet than walking all the steps to the park, which is at track level and much higher than the road. Brian Solomon

Above: Finding the right road out of Altoona to reach the Horseshoe Curve can be a bit of a challenge, but once you head up Burgoon Run there's no missing the famous curve. Brian Solomon

The railroad's first obstacle to reaching Pittsburgh was bridging the Susquehanna north of Harrisburg at Rockville. This feat was accomplished with a multiple-span wooden Howe truss in 1849. By using portions of the Portage Railroad to surmount the Alleghenies, PRR formed a through-route to Pittsburgh in 1852. By 1855, PRR opened its own mountain line via the Horseshoe Curve (see below) to Pittsburgh. The new line reduced transit time from Philadelphia to Pittsburgh from four to five days via the Main Line of Public Works to 13 hours by express train.

Unlike the Main Line of Public Works, which stagnated after reaching its initial goal, PRR continued to grow and grow. It extended lines up the valleys and towns to eventually dominate Pennsylvania transport west of the Susquehanna River. PRR built, bought, and leased more and more lines, adding existing and proposed railroads to its system. Among the most significant of these were the Northern Central, which built north from Baltimore and followed the Susquehanna north of Harrisburg; the Philadelphia & Erie, chartered to build west from Sunbury (finally in 1864 reaching the city of Erie, via Renovo and Emporium with PRR's backing); and the Cumberland Valley Railroad that extended southwesterly from Harrisburg toward Hagerstown, Maryland.

In 1857, PRR bought the Main Line of Public Works from the state. By that time, the archaic network had completely lost its ability to compete. Most valuable to PRR was the Philadelphia & Columbia, which had effectively served as PRR's eastward connection. The old Belmont Plane was long abandoned by that time; the

The Pennsylvania Railroad expanded its empire rapidly during the middle of the nineteenth century. Among the lines it acquired were the Northern Central and Philadelphia & Erie. These lines met here at Sunbury, along the east bank of the Susquehanna River. In later years, this was on PRR's route from Baltimore to Buffalo. Emerging from the fog in October 2003, the Juniata Terminal Company E8As are seen with an excursion passing Sunbury on the way to the old PRR shop town of Renovo. Brian Solomon

all-rail route had been in place since about 1840.

PRR didn't miss a beat to seek out new traffic. When oil was discovered near Titusville in northwestern Pennsylvania in 1859, PRR was among the lines that tapped the gush of oil traffic in the mid-1860s and reached the area with its Allegheny Valley line.

Although its charter focused PRR on Pennsylvania routes, the railroad's builders watched anxiously as Vanderbilt's New York Central, the Erie Railroad, and B&O developed parallel trunks between East Coast ports and Midwest gateways. To counter these projects, PRR wasted little time in securing its own western arms and rapidly developed as one of the four major east-west truck lines. After bridging the Allegheny River in 1858, PRR reached Chicago through its Pittsburgh, Fort Wayne & Chicago Railway affiliate in 1859. During the 1860s, PRR struggled to maintain its western connections and ultimately leased two parallel Pittsburgh–Chicago routes, with its famed Panhandle Line serving as a southern route and the Fort Wayne as the northern.

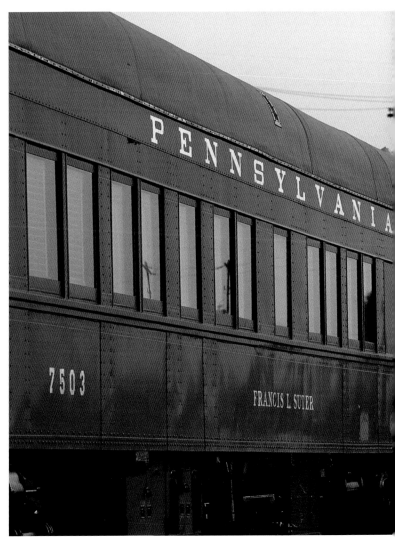

Top: The Philadelphia & Columbia was built as part of the Main Line of Public Works to connect its namesake cities. The line became integral to the Pennsylvania Railroad as its primary route east of Harrisburg. The PRR acquired the line from the state in 1857and electrified it in 1939. Until the advent of Conrail in 1976, this was operated as both an important freight and passenger route with four main tracks over much of the route. Today, it primarily serves as a passenger line, with infrequent Norfolk Southern freights using it largely to serve local customers. On a May evening at Gap, an Amtrak Keystone service races eastward under wire powered by an AEM-7 electric. Brian Solomon

Right: In its heyday during the first decades of the twentieth century, the Pennsylvania Railroad was more than just the most important railroad in the commonwealth. It was the largest transportation company in the world. It was the single largest mover of freight, and it carried the largest number of passengers of any North American railroad. PRR's officers were the titans of industry and traveled in a style befitting their position. This 1914-built Pullman was used by various PRR officers in their travels around the system. Brian Solomon

Philadelphia had been the focus of the PRR's early charter, but raw economics and its need to secure territory and traffic from its competitors resulted in the railroad acquiring control of lines from New York to Washington, D.C. By the end of the century, PRR was the largest and busiest railroad in the nation with main lines connecting myriad points from New York, Philadelphia, Baltimore, and Washington to Chicago and St. Louis, and from Baltimore to Buffalo and Rochester with tracks radiating throughout Pennsylvania and the Midwest.

With ever increasing traffic and healthy profits, railroad management continually improved the road's lines. These measures included straightening curves, making nominal line relocations to improve grades, and adding main-line tracks. As a result, PRR's main line across Pennsylvania developed as the most intense avenue of commerce in the country. By 1900, it was known as Broad Way because of its broad, four-track line (not to be confused for either the Erie's broad gauge or New York City's famous street). The growing industrial complex around Pittsburgh and surrounding valleys tied to steel manufacturing fueled PRR's lines in the region. Central and western Pennsylvania remained the heart of the railroad, even though its offices were seated in Philadelphia.

Horseshoe Curve

The most spectacular and most famous section of railroad in Pennsylvania is the Horseshoe Curve—so-named because its outline as seen on a map or viewed from above resembles the shape of a common horseshoe. Ensconced in Burgoon Run, a magnificent idyllic valley west of Altoona, the Curve is the site of daily struggle as enormous mile long freight trains fight to reach the summit of the Alleghenies. Constructed in 1854 when the PRR was pushing its all-rail route westward to reach Pittsburgh, the curve was Thomson's clever engineering solution to the railroad's most serious grade problem.

Thomson's thorough knowledge of railroad operations enabled him to have a level of understanding that eluded all but a few men in those formative years of railroad building. His route deviated from earlier surveys, which forced a line in the mountains much sooner than necessary, because he understood that it would be cheaper to both build and operate a railroad that featured a short but steeply graded line, rather than that

In this stereograph view from the 1870s, a 4-4-0 runs engine-light ahead of an eastward freight descending the Horseshoe Curve. This was before the third and fourth tracks were added, prior to the point when the railroad decided to manicure the curve. With its undergrowth, narrow right-of-way, and lack of ballast, the famous curve looks quite different from its modern appearance. In addition, there isn't a railroad enthusiast in sight! Railroad Museum of Pennsylvania PHMC

In 1985, K4s No. 1361, which had been displayed at Horseshoe Curve since the 1950s, was removed for restoration; in its place a former PRR GP9 No. 7048 was displayed. Where the K4s was significant to the PRR as the backbone of its passenger fleet, the Electro-Motive GP9 has national significance as the most common type of diesel-electric of the steam-to-diesel transition period. The GP9 enabled PRR to retire its last steam locomotives, and thousands of these mass-produced locomotives worked lines from Maine to Mexico. Today, visitors may inspect this solid old machine delivered to the PRR in 1955. Brian Solomon

favored by early surveys that used a prolonged but moderately graded line. His line followed a circuitous water level route along the Susquehanna and Juniata rivers as far as present-day Altoona. From there, it began its serious climb across the Allegheny Divide.

Driving through in the Valley of Burgoon Run, the novice might wonder why Thomson didn't simply bridge the valley here or construct a tall fill instead of detouring the tracks deep into the valley and up the other side. But this detour with the Horseshoe Curve was key to his whole strategy. To maintain a steady climb without facing an insurmountable gradient, Thomson laid this great sweeping horseshoe that winds toward Kittanning Point. Beyond the curve, the railroad continues its climb and finally crests the Allegheny Divide in tunnels bored through the ridge at Gallitzin.

Built for double track, Horseshoe Curve became famous not just for its picturesque track arrangement, but for its heavy volume of traffic that over the years required expansion to three and ultimately to four main tracks by 1900. Although a great many horseshoe curves were constructed on railroads across the world, this remains the grandest and most elegant of all.

At the zenith of PRR operations, its lines across the Allegheny Divide handled more than 100 trains daily. Many were coal, ore, and merchandise freights for which the railroad was famous—trains that required big steam locomotives fore and aft to pull and shove tonnage up the grade. Yet, this was a major passenger corridor as well. The May 1921 *Official Guide of the Railways* lists no less than 24 scheduled passenger trains weekdays around the curve. These trains included PRR's famous New York–Chicago first-class all-sleeper extra-fare *Broadway Limited,* the less well-known

This PRR-styled sign on the side of The Tunnel Inn ensures that visitors know where they are. Brian Solomon

Phillipsburg–Pittsburgh *Lehigh Pennsylvania Express*, along with named trains such as *The New Yorker*, *Manhattan Limited*, and *Buckeye Limited*, as well as 12 nameless overnight trains, seven nameless through day trains, and five all-stop local services.

After World War II, ridership dropped off steadily, and through the 1950s and 1960s PRR curtailed many trains. By the time Conrail assumed operation of the line from Penn Central in 1976, passenger traffic had dwindled. By then, Amtrak operated passenger services that provided only a few daily trains on this line. Although freight traffic remained robust, the loss of most passenger trains resulted in fewer moves over the line. When Conrail was faced with trimming the railroad system to cut costs in the 1980s, Horseshoe Curve was targeted. Improved signaling and changes in freight operations made it possible to lift one of the four lines by making the middle track bidirectional. In 1981, Conrail ripped up the old No. 2 track over the mountain and left just three tracks in place. The remnant of the New Portage Railroad around the so-called Muleshoe Curve was also abandoned at about the same time. East of Altoona, the line was reduced to two main tracks with bidirectional signaling.

However, the line still remains one of the busiest freight lines in the East, accommodating 50 to 60 heavy trains daily. Since 1999, Norfolk Southern has operated the line. As of 2007, a few old diesels were still in Conrail blue paint, but most on the line were in shiny, Norfolk Southern black.

From the ridge at Tunnel Hill above Gallitzin is this panoramic view looking down Sugar Run. On an early November morning, a Norfolk Southern coal train is slowly descending the steeply graded track from the Portage Tunnel. The locomotives pictured are helpers at the back of the train that are needed to assist by providing dynamic braking to help ensure the train does not descend too quickly.
Brian Solomon

Visitors to the Horseshoe Curve rarely have to wait long for something to pass. In addition to the 50-plus freights that use the line daily, frequent light helpers often move over the line. Here, a set of Electro-Motive SD40-2s—built in the 1970s—glides downgrade toward Altoona. The volume of heavy traffic around Horseshoe Curve may require five or more helper sets on duty at any one time. Helpers may be used at the front, back, or, on rare occasions, in the middle of freight trains to assist them upgrade. In some cases—when extra braking is needed— helpers may be used downgrade. Since helper locomotives and crews are based at Cresson, it is not unusual to find light helper engines running in either direction for positioning or to return them to their base. Brian Solomon

Cresson is one of several communities on the west slope of Norfolk Southern's former Pennsylvania Railroad Main Line that caters to railroad enthusiasts. A railroad park has been built along Front Street and across the track from the helper terminal. All along this street are places to watch and enjoy the continuous procession of freight trains. At the west end of the street is the ever-popular Station Inn bed and breakfast. Brian Solomon

The borough of Cassandra, located a few miles west of Cresson, is another excellent place to experience heavy modern main-line railroading. This view of a westward Norfolk Southern intermodal train led by an SD70 diesel-electric is from the manicured Railroad Overlook just east of the fire station. Here, Norfolk Southern's triple-track main line accommodates upwards of 50 heavy freights daily, as well as hosts Amtrak's Pennsylvanian. *Brian Solomon*

Visiting Horseshoe Curve

Splendid Appalachian scenery and the ability to watch a long train for several minutes as it struggles up the grade, combined with the large number of trains passing by, are the reasons why Horseshoe Curve is one of America's premier train-watching venues. First landscaped in 1879, the site now has a visitor's park that provides a majestic vantage point for the public to enjoy the sight of trains grinding up and down the mountain.

At the end of the steam era, PRR placed one of its famous K4s Pacifics on display in the park. This display represented the role that the locomotive type had played for 40 years hauling the company's passenger trains, which had put it among America's most famous steam locomotives. In the 1980s, the K4s was removed from its perch on the curve and briefly restored to working condition.

In its place, a venerable GP9 diesel-electric was installed, and this diesel remains on display to this day. Built by General Motors Electro-Motive Division in the 1950s to replace steam, the GP9 was a common type for many years. Groups of them worked the front and back of heavy PRR freights. Although they were much louder than today's diesels, this old GP9 had a horsepower rating of just 1,750 horsepower. Most of the diesels on the line today are rated at 4,000 horsepower or higher, but they are equipped with mufflers to reduce noise output and squelch their roar somewhat.

In 1992, the visitor's center for the Horseshoe Curve National Historic Landmark was dramatically overhauled, upgraded, and remodeled. At this time, a short funicular railway was installed to bring visitors to track level. This electrically operated cable line is reminiscent of the inclined planes on the old Allegheny

An eastward Norfolk Southern intermodal train catches the evening sun as it ascends the west slope at Portage. Much of the freight that now moves over the former Pennsylvania Railroad Main Line is handled in containerized intermodal shipments.
Brian Solomon

Portage line that Horseshoe Curve replaced. Visitors who want to get a bit of exercise may opt to walk the 194 steps up to track level. There is a nominal charge to visit the site.

Although the railroad is the main attraction, it is well worth a visit to the interpretive center, which helps put the famous curve in perspective. A scaled diorama allows visitors to appreciate Thomson's engineering. When viewing this model, remember that Thomson engineered the curve by surveying it from the ground at the time when Burgoon Run was little more than wilderness. Among the displays are models of Pennsylvania Railroad trains that traversed the line in the railroad's golden age. Also spot the bottle of Curve Beer, which was brewed locally in Altoona.

Horseshoe Curve is a place that many railroad enthusiasts aim to visit at least once in their life, but many make repeated trips. The center even sells annual passes for the frequent visitor. Beyond Horseshoe Curve, the line winds into the valley of Sugar Run and continuously climbs to the summit of the Allegheny Divide. At MG Tower—old telegraph initials that infer "mid-grade"—are a complete set of crossovers, allowing trains to cross from one main track to another, which increases the flexibility and thus the capacity of the line. Traditionally, the crossovers were operated from the old brick tower built in the style of a classic Swiss chalet, but today they are normally operated remotely by Norfolk Southern's dispatcher in Pittsburgh.

Gallitzin

Traditionally, the PRR had three tunnels beneath the Allegheny Divide. The west portals of the northernmost tunnels are on a parallel alignment, and they are located in the village, exiting the mountain in a deep earth cutting. New Portage Tunnel is on a separate alignment that is a short distance south of village. Today, only two of the three tunnels at Gallitzin carry tracks.

In the mid-1990s, with the help of state funds, Conrail improved the overhead clearances on the former

Amtrak's Pennsylvanian *works upgrade at Summerhill on a bright September morning. Summerhill has manicured the area around the signal bridge and has provided parking for railroad enthusiasts to watch trains. Among the attractions is the signal bridge itself, which as of 2007 still carried vintage Pennsylvania Railroad position light signals. In PRR days, it would have been unfathomable for the railroad to have even considered using colored lights. Yet, today this type of signal is standard, while the old position light style is on the wane.* Brian Solomon

PRR Main Line. The road widened the Allegheny Tunnel to carry two main tracks, while removing track from the northernmost Gallitzin Tunnel. The latter bore survives as an access road.

Visitors to Gallitzin may view trains exiting the west portal of the Allegheny Tunnel from a road bridge conveniently situated several hundred feet west of the portals. Another viewing point is from the nearby Tunnel Park on the north side of the cutting. Heavy freights struggling uphill are often preceded by exhaust that will pour forth from the portal. Today, both westward and eastward trains use this tunnel, while the bore on the south side of town is normally reserved for eastward moves because of the unusually steep gradient beyond the east portal known as The Slide.

The Tunnel Park and Museum features several prominent exhibits, including the preserved PRR

N5C cabin car No. 477852 that is located in sight of the tracks. This car is often staffed by volunteers. The Pennsylvania Railroad had always referred to its cabooses as cabin cars—a term that accurately reflected its traditional role as the office, bunkhouse, and tail car that was attached to most freight trains. Among the more unusual models was the N5C, which featured pairs of circular windows at each end and on each side of the car.

Conrail, like most American railroads, phased out the use of cabooses in the mid-1980s. This change was made possible by the widespread use of train radio, combined with new technology to monitor brake-line air pressure using telemetry equipment, as well as the reduction of crew sizes and revision to work rules. Today, most freight trains operate without cabooses, and all crew-members ride on the locomotive(s).

One need not travel too far to find accommodation in Gallitzin. On the south side of the cutting, and within sight of the tunnels, is The Tunnel Inn bed and breakfast. This B&B specializes in catering to visiting railroad enthusiasts.

Cresson

This top-of-the-mountain yard is where the helper locomotives are based and serviced. The town of Cresson has grown up around the railroad, with most of the main streets running parallel to the old PRR tracks south of the main line.

Two coal branches meet the main line here; until the 1990s, the town was the location of MO Tower, a classic structure. The tower was eliminated as part of a resignaling project that was conducted in conjunction with clearance improvements. Also removed was a grade-separated flyover, which crossed the main line

just east of the helper base and that had allowed coal trains coming off the Cresson secondary line to join the main line in the eastward direction without interfering with westward traffic. A train viewing park and elevated deck have been established in town along the main line opposite the helper base. Another PRR N5C cabin car is displayed here.

A popular railroad-themed bed and breakfast called the Station Inn is situated a few blocks railroad-west of the park along the main line.

Lilly, Cassandra, and Beyond

The valley between Lilly and South Fork features a variety of overlapping abandoned railroad alignments, in addition to the busy three-track former PRR Main Line. The latter is characterized by long tangents constructed in the late nineteenth century and early twentieth century that eliminated Thomson's original sinuous

A November view of Johnstown's historic inclined railway. Opened in 1891, the double-track incline uses cars large enough to accept automobiles. These are lifted and lowered simultaneously on opposite tracks using heavy steel cables. Although the incline is much steeper than those once used by the Allegheny Portage Railroad, the basic concept is the same. The line is just over 867 feet long.
Brian Solomon

alignment. This change was a result of the complicated history of railroad operations on the west slope. Careful study will reveal the alignments of the Portage Railroad and its inclined planes, the New Portage Railroad, and older PRR main-line alignments—some of which have been used to tap various bituminous coal mines over the years or converted into local roads, including portions of Highway 53.

West of Cresson, the main line descends through the villages of Lilly and Cassandra. Lilly, like Cresson, has streets built parallel to the tracks. The sweeping curve southwest of the village has been a popular place to take dramatic photographs of uphill trains. A few miles farther west, the borough of Cassandra maintains a Railfan Welcome Center, where visitors are encouraged to sign a guestbook. Those curious about the earlier railway alignments will find a historic, detailed map here. However, Cassandra's main attraction is its railroad overlook just to the east of the village, at the site of an old overhead bridge. This bucolic setting has been landscaped with photographers in mind, and benches are set up at convenient angles for train watchers. To the east of Cassandra Overlook, the line climbs toward the summit in a broad sweeping curve,

while to the west of the bridge, the railroad bisects a deep rock cut located at the beginning of a long tangent. From the bridge, you can watch a heavy eastward train struggle for several miles with its locomotives in full throttle and helpers shoving hard on the back.

The three main tracks are put to good use. It is not unusual to find a faster, eastward train on the middle overtake a slower one in the race to the summit. If you're lucky, you might get three trains passing at once! Cassandra may be best reached by taking Route 53 west from Lilly. The village is on the north side of the present main line. The old main line made an S-bend, which defined the town's alignment prior to construction of the deep cutting. Farther down the hill at Portage, Summerhill, and South Fork are a variety of places to watch this busy railroad at work. Nearby Johnstown features a well-maintained former PRR passenger station, a park facing the multiple arch bridge over the Little Conemaugh River (the earlier bridge at this location was famous for its role in Johnstown's great flood of 1889), and a historic funicular railway. Ride this line to the top of the hill for an outstanding view of the bridge and valley below.

The view from the top of the incline is excellent for train watching. Here, a westward Norfolk Southern intermodal train winds through the industrial confines of the Conemaugh River Valley. Brian Solomon

ALTOONA RAILROADERS MEMORIAL MUSEUM By John Gruber

The Pennsylvania Railroad was the largest corporation of early twentieth-century America when it was described by *Fortune* magazine in 1936 as "a nation unto itself." In the 1850s, PRR selected this Juniata Valley location as the site for its major shops. Over the next century, it designed, built, tested, maintained, and repaired its machines of transportation here. The strategic location near the base of its Allegheny crossing was then near the mid-point of its operating system.

Altoona has long been a popular place for train watchers. It is located just off Interstate Highway 99, and it is a hub of the area's growing tourist industry. The city itself has many significant cultural resources, and most of these resources link directly to the city's long history as a railroad center. Allegheny Portage Railroad National Historic Site, Johnstown Flood National Memorial, Horseshoe Curve National Historic Site, Staple Bend Tunnel, and the historic iron furnace at Mount Etna are all within 25 miles of Altoona. Altoona also hosts one of Pennsylvania's most significant railroad museums.

Altoona's long and proud association with the railroad industry has made it a prime site for a first-class railroad museum. Roughly 17,000 people were employed at the Pennsylvania Railroad's Altoona Works during its peak years in the 1920s. The museum, located at 1300 Ninth Avenue in the former master mechanics building, is full of displays about work and play in the central Pennsylvania city. The museum opened in 1980. It celebrated the renovation of the master mechanics building and installation of its interpretative exhibits in 1998. Its goal is ambitious: commemorating and celebrating the significant contributions of railroaders and their families to American life and industry.

The exhibits describe the massive 217-acre industrial complex that operated in Altoona in its heyday, as well as home and social life in the city. As you enter the narrow, three-story building, you will see sculptured figures working on a partial replica of Pennsylvania Railroad locomotive No. 1361, the most famous of PRR's K4s Pacific-type passenger locomotives built in Altoona. No. 1361 and the figures honor the workers who produced 6,783 steam locomotives in 100 years and rebuilt 150 locomotives per month. You can sit in Kelly's Bar, a replication of a typical Altoona tavern and hear recreated railroaders and townspeople talk about the day's activities.

Altoona remains a railroad town. From the museum, you can walk across a pedestrian bridge that spans the busy, multiple-track Norfolk Southern main line to the Amtrak station and downtown Altoona. Although it is much reduced in size from the PRR days, as of 2007 the Norfolk Southern operates a major locomotive repair shop in a few of the PRR buildings.

PART IV
RAILWAYS LARGE AND SMALL

Although Pennsylvania is best known for the vast and intensive operations of the former Pennsylvania Railroad and the myriad of old anthracite haulers east of the Susquehanna, it has also been served by a number of other railroads, large and small. These have ranged from the old New York Central System and Baltimore & Ohio Railroad to one-time regional narrow-gauge coal haulers, such as the East Broad Top.

Each of these railroads began operating in Pennsylvania for a different purpose, and their present-day roles also vary greatly. Where much of New York Central's lines in the state have been fragmented, the old B&O main line is now a key component of CSX's freight network and hosts Amtrak's Washington D.C.–Chicago *Capitol Limited*. In Pittsburgh, it's hard to travel through the Steel City and not see a train moving somewhere. In addition to freight main lines operated by Norfolk Southern, CSX, and Bessemer & Lake Erie, two historic incline railways operate here, as does the PAT light-rail system.

Big time main-line railroading has only been part of the story in this state. Among the most significant, but smaller, excursion lines is the privately run East Broad Top. Because of its historic appearance and equipment (much of it saved from the scrapper), this one-time coal-hauling line has been transformed into a much-loved tourist attraction. Also, the quaint Pennsylvania Trolley Museum at Washington is one of the nation's best presented museums of electric railway equipment and features heavy-rail rarities—including the oldest operating diesel-electric and a rare former New York, Ontario & Western caboose.

Pennsylvania's railway heritage is so rich and complex that it could take a lifetime to fully explore. While some of its railways and sites are covered in detail in this book, many others are just touched upon to give readers a sense for the diversity and number of sites found in the commonwealth.

Tioga Central's excursion train, led by a vintage Alco RS1 diesel, departs Wellsboro Junction on its northward run passing a stored Tioga Central Alco S-2 switcher. Both locomotives are painted in a neo–Lehigh Valley livery. Brian Solomon

CHAPTER 12

NEW YORK CENTRAL LINES

One of the earliest transportation systems in the region of Tioga County, Pennsylvania, was initiated in 1828 by the Tioga Coal, Iron Mining, and Manufacturing Company. The company envisioned adapting the Tioga River into a canal to provide practical shipping up to its confluence with the Chemung River, near present-day Corning, New York. By 1833, this system had evolved into a primitive railroad scheme with the intention of connecting Corning with Blossburg, Pennsylvania.

Over the next half-century, a series of short railways were built reaching from Corning to Jersey Shore, Pennsylvania. In the early years, these fed the Erie Railroad, which had been built across New York's Southern Tier in the 1850s. In the late nineteenth century, additional lines were built farther north into New York State and were ultimately consolidated by the Fall Brook Coal Company into what became the Fall Brook Railway. The scenic highlight of this route was the line south of Wellsboro Junction that traversed the deep and narrow defile along Pine Creek, known as the Grand Canyon of Pennsylvania.

In its original configuration, Cornelius Vanderbilt's New York Central did not tap coal fields. In the last decades of the nineteenth century, Central took a keen interest in bituminous coal regions of central Pennsylvania. Its logic was obvious, since these coal fields were closest to its main trunk line. Among the properties Central invested in were the Beech Creek Railroad, which had built in the coal-producing Clearfield District, and the Fall Brook. The latter, with its extensions north from Corning to Geneva and Lyons, New York, made direct connections with New York Central. In the mid-1880s, New York Central was nearly forced to give up its interest in the Beech Creek Railroad as a result of J. P. Morgan's settlement regarding the South Penn Railroad (discussed later in this chapter). However,

Facing page: This July 9, 1958, view of the Duquesne Incline looks down toward the Monongahela River. The tracks directly below were those of the Pennsylvania Railroad, while those at the bottom were Pittsburgh & Lake Erie's. This incline is one of two surviving inclined railways in Pittsburgh. Richard Jay Solomon

Above: Station Square Freight House Shops are adjacent to the former P&LE offices and passenger terminal, across the street from the historic cable-hauled Monongahela Incline, as well as a station on Pittsburgh's PAT light-rail line. Visitors may ride the incline up the side of Mount Washington for a nominal fee; the views of Pittsburgh from the ridge are well worth the price. This area is steeped in railroad history and has a great variety of active rail lines—from the inclined railways to CSX and Norfolk Southern heavy freight main lines. Brian Solomon

Central retained its control of the Beech Creek and formally leased it in 1890. To tap the Beech Creek, Central expanded its interest in the Fall Brook and leased the line from 1899. Central also pushed a low-grade route westward across the commonwealth to connect with its lines in Ohio.

For much of the twentieth century, New York Central operated these lines and used them to haul bituminous coal, including that used as fuel for its steam locomotives. Central operated substantial yards at Clearfield and Jersey Shore, and it maintained connections at the latter with the Reading Company. These lines continued as coal conduits into the Penn Central era. The Fall Brook route was favored by PC over the former PRR Elmira branch, which was largely dismembered after damages incurred from Hurricane Agnes in 1972.

Agnes caused several crucial changes to the Fall Brook route as well. The railroad was realigned through Corning, New York, as a direct result of flooding. The old Fall Brook joined the former Erie at Gang Mills for a few miles in place of its own alignment. In the wake of Agnes, area officials constructed a flood control dam in Tioga County that resulted in the relocation of several miles of the Fall Brook line.

Conrail took over in 1976, and as late as 1988, it operated through-unit coal trains from central Pennsylvania, as well as through freights. Three times a week, Conrail's ENSY/SYEN symbol manifest freight ran between Dewitt Yard near Syracuse, New York, and the former PRR Enola Yards opposite Harrisburg. Conrail severed the line between Wellsboro Junction and a point near Jersey Shore in 1988. The company lifted the rails and left the Grand Canyon of Pennsylvania without tracks. Today, much of this route hosts the 57-mile-long Pine Creek Rail-Trail that runs from Ansonia to Jersey Shore. The scenic splendor of this route has made it among the most popular rail-trails (rail lines converted to bike trails) in the region. The coal trains may be just a memory, but at least the old right-of-way has been put to good use.

In 1992, Conrail spun off the remainder of the line below Corning to short-line operator Wellsboro & Corning, which has provided local freight service ever since. Former New York Central lines in the vicinity of Clearfield were sold to short-line railway operator R. J. Corman in the mid-1990s. This line is difficult to appreciate because the tracks are largely shrouded by trees and difficult to access, and trains are relatively infrequent.

One of the most popular ways to travel the old Fall Brook route is on a Tioga Central excursion train. On a crisp October afternoon, the northward excursion plods along the line once used by coal trains and other freight. Although never an important passenger line, the Fall Brook hosted several daily passenger trains in the late-nineteenth century. Brian Solomon

After Conrail abandoned the Fall Brook route south of Wellsboro Junction, the old line through the Grand Canyon of Pennsylvania was transformed into the 57-mile-long Pine Creek Rail-Trail. In 1894, Fall Brook Railway's scheduled southward passenger train, No. 1, departed Lyons, New York, at 7 A.M., paused at Stokesdale Junction—as Wellsboro Junction was then known—between 11:50 A.M. and noon, and arrived in Williamsport at 3:20 P.M. Connections via the Philadelphia & Reading were available with a 10:10 P.M. arrival at Philadelphia's Reading Terminal. Thom Kinard

Riding the Fall Brook

Since 1994, Tioga Central has provided seasonal passenger excursions over Wellsboro & Corning between Wellsboro Junction and Hammond Lake—the post-Agnes flood control creation. Excursions are typically operated from Wellsboro using streamlined passenger cars hauled by historic Alco diesels over the route once known as a conduit for coal. Prior to Tioga Central, the line had not regularly hosted passenger trains for years because the later New York Central, Penn Central, and Conrail periods were predominantly freight operations.

Although the right-of-way through the Grand Canyon of Pennsylvania is now just a trail in the woods, Tioga Central's excursion offers passengers unique views of northcentral Pennsylvania.

Pittsburgh & Lake Erie

By the 1870s, Pittsburgh was a well developed Pennsylvania Railroad stronghold, and PRR's lines radiated out to serve the region's growing steel industry. Baltimore & Ohio had finally penetrated this crucible of PRR traffic in the early part of the decade, so when the new Pittsburgh & Lake Erie was chartered in 1875, it anticipated allying itself with B&O as a means of defying PRR's near monopoly. But in 1877, instead of B&O, P&LE attracted the Vanderbilts' interest as a way to tap lucrative Pittsburgh-area traffic.

By 1889, the New York Central had control of P&LE, and it remained a key component of the New York Central System through the NYC merger with PRR in 1968. Initially, P&LE's main line connected its namesake city with Youngstown, Ohio, and it attained its classic shape with an extension reaching Connellsville and McKeesport to Brownsville Junction. Connellsville was known for ample deposits of coal and coke, but perhaps as important to P&LE when it completed this line in 1883 were the Vanderbilts' interests in building the fabled South Penn Railroad. Although the South Penn

An eastward CSX freight rolls along the former Pittsburgh & Lake Erie line on the west bank of the Monongahela, beneath the famous Fort Pitt bowstring arch bridge, passing Station Square in the former P&LE buildings opposite downtown Pittsburgh. This photograph was taken from Gustav Lindenthal's famous Smithfield Street Bridge over the Monongahela (that once carried Pittsburgh trolleys), just a short walk from a host of railway sites in the area. Brian Solomon

came to naught, P&LE's Connellsville line provided a convenient connection with Western Maryland when that line extended west from Cumberland, Maryland, in 1912.

P&LE's water-level profile served the heavy industrialized Pittsburgh region, where miles of steel mills, forges, and foundries left little doubt as to what its trains carried. In addition to tens of thousands of tons of ore, coke, and limestone used in the making of steel, P&LE was also a major hauler of bituminous (soft) coal. Its compact system (Pittsburgh to Youngstown was just 65 miles, and the whole P&LE consisted of only 223 route miles in 1952) and relatively short haul yielded an enormous volume of freight traffic, which resulting in P&LE's well-known nickname, "Little Giant."

What was unusual to the system were the railroad's numerous short-line subsidiaries that fed freight traffic to its main lines. The specifics of control and ownership varied from line to line. Its closely held subsidiaries included the Montour, the Pittsburgh, Chartiers & Youghiogheny—known colloquially as the Peachy Wye—and Youngstown & Southern. Among its most significant feeders was the Monongahela Railway, a line that in 1952 operated 178 miles of line and was capable of moving 7,500-ton trains. It was jointly owned by P&LE, B&O, and PRR, and it fed rivers of bituminous coal to all three railroads.

P&LE melded into Penn Central in 1968, but its fate took an unusual twist after its parent declared bankruptcy in 1970. The line fought inclusion in Conrail and remained a Penn Central subsidiary through 1979, when it regained independence. For a few years, it enjoyed robust freight traffic. However, while the collapse of the eastern railroad industry in the early 1970s enabled P&LE to regain its independence, the collapse of Pittsburgh's steel industry in the late 1970s and early 1980s doomed the line. Between

Intended to rival the opulence of the PRR's nearby structures, Pittsburgh & Lake Erie's passenger terminal and office building exuded an ornate style associated with the corporate wealth of the early twentieth century. P&LE was among the most lucrative parts of the New York Central system. Designed by architect William G. Burns, the terminal building was completed in 1901 and adapted in the early 1980s as part of the Station Square complex. The building still stands along the old P&LE main line. Although it no longer serves as either a station or an office for the railroad, long CSX freights glide by more than a dozen times daily. Brian Solomon

The old Pittsburgh & Lake Erie freight house in Pittsburgh is one of five former railroad structures adapted as Station Square, including the upscale shopping mall appropriately known as Freight House Shops. The building retains elements of its railroad heritage while serving in its new role. The restored clerestory roof is evident in this interior view. Brian Solomon

1980 and 1984, its tonnage halved. By the mid-1980s, P&LE was surviving on coal traffic and payments from CSX—corporate successor to the B&O—which utilized 58 miles of trackage rights on P&LE between McKeesport and New Castle Junction. This agreement had been in place since 1934 and provided B&O with a more efficient route through Pittsburgh in order to avoid sending freight over its own steeply graded Pittsburgh & Western line.

P&LE floundered for a few more years. Much of its once-busy line had become a rusty shadow, and its connection with Western Maryland was dry (as a result of that line being absorbed into CSX predecessor Chessie System). The decaying steel plants along its lines served as stark reminders as to where the rest of the traffic had gone. CSX, looking to secure its B&O route in the

region, absorbed the remainder of P&LE in 1992. In a sense, the P&LE came full circle as it finally had joined the B&O network.

Station Square

Pittsburgh & Lake Erie's crown jewel and its public face was its Pittsburgh terminal, an opulent building constructed between 1899 and 1901 along the west bank of the Monongahela opposite downtown Pittsburgh. This location served as both its main passenger terminal and its main offices. Since P&LE's terminal sat at the heart of the Pennsylvania Railroad's empire, no expense was spared to show up the competition. The building was designed by architect William G. Burns. While conservative classical motifs characterize its exterior, the building's interior shows off like a gilded peacock.

Although P&LE served as a virtual conveyor belt for steel industries, which traditionally provided roughly 75 percent of its freight traffic, P&LE also operated a fleet of passenger trains between Pittsburgh, Youngstown, and beyond. Best known was the *Empire Express*, which provided a daytime service to Buffalo and carried sleeping cars to Albany and Massena, New York, and Boston. Nameless services directly connected Pittsburgh with Cleveland, Detroit, and Toronto. Passengers could also reach Chicago, Indianapolis, and St. Louis. As late as 1949, P&LE had a dozen daily departures from this Pittsburgh terminal. Since B&O's through trains graced P&LE's tracks and some of its long-distance trains had also been stopping here since 1934, the famous all-Pullman *Capitol Limited*, *The Washingtonian*, and the *Columbian* paused for passengers here as well.

By the founding of Amtrak in 1971, P&LE's days as a long-distance passenger carrier were behind it. However, it continued to operate a daily commuter train between Pittsburgh and College Station at Beaver Falls. Despite exceptional losses, P&LE operated this classic train with a single GP7 diesel and streamlined passenger cars until 1984.

Appreciation for the great buildings of the railroads' golden age waned in the 1960s and 1970s. While many great stations faced the wrecking ball, P&LE's Pittsburgh terminal was adapted into a splendid public venue. It became Station Square, thanks largely to the efforts of Pittsburgh History & Landmarks Foundation. Over time, Station Square has become host to trendy shops and restaurants. It is now advertised as Pittsburgh's most popular tourist attraction. Most visitors come for the atmosphere, views of the Pittsburgh

Mount Washington above Station Square affords a panoramic view of Pittsburgh and a host of railroad interest. Seen in the foreground is the former Pennsylvania Railroad Monongahela River Bridge—commonly known as the Panhandle Bridge for PRR's Pittsburgh, Cincinnati & St. Louis subsidiary that operated as the Panhandle Railroad. This bridge is now used for PAT light-rail instead of heavy railroad trains. The river itself is a transportation corridor, serving both freight barges and pleasure craft. CSX's former P&LE main line and a Norfolk Southern former PRR line on the west bank of the river are also visible from this overlook near the top of the Monongahela Incline. Brian Solomon

While mostly known for coal trains in northcentral Pennsylvania, R. J. Corman handles general merchandise business on more than 300 miles of track in the Keystone State. A westbound train powered by six R. J. Corman GP38s rolls along the banks of the Susquehanna River at Rolling Stone, Pennsylvania, on a hazy summer morning heading for Clearfield. This train was collected from the Norfolk Southern interchange along the old PRR Buffalo Line at Keating. Scott R. Snell

skyline, and the shopping. On top of that, Station Square is a great place to watch trains and enjoy railroad heritage. P&LE may be a memory, but its classic terminal survives. Its tracks still host CSX through freights, which pass from time to time en route to yards at Cumberland, Maryland, and New Castle, Pennsylvania, and beyond. Nearby Norfolk Southern trains use former PRR tracks.

Station Square may be reached by car, by foot, or by Pittsburgh's light-rail transit system—which evolved from its old electric trolley network. Today, light-rail vehicles cross the Monongahela on the old PRR Panhandle Bridge

near the P&LE station. Visitors will be interested in the Monongahela Incline, one of two surviving funicular railways in Pittsburgh. This incline was built in 1870, and it takes passengers to the ridge overlooking the station. From here, you can see spectacular views of the skyline, as well as the old P&LE main line. Farther down the river, the tunnel once used by the Pittsburgh & West Virginia to reach its Pittsburgh passenger station is now a highway tunnel. The railroad bridge piers are an indication of where the tracks once crossed the river. Beyond this is Pittsburgh's other surviving funicular, the famed Duquesne Incline, which is also in sight of Station Square.

Western Maryland 0-6-0 No. 1008 leads a nine-car freight at Porters, Pennsylvania, in 1946. Western Maryland operated several lines in southern portions of the commonwealth. Together with several other lines, Western Maryland served as an alternative east-west trunk line known as the Alphabet Route. Much of the WM was parallel to the Baltimore & Ohio's main line, and it was melded into the Chessie System in the 1970s. Portions of its trackage in eastern Pennsylvania are still operated by CSX and short lines, but most of its main line to Connellsville was abandoned and now serves as a popular rail-trail. Norris R. Young Thomas T. Taber Collection, Railroad Museum of Pennsylvania PHMC

CHAPTER 13

EAST BROAD TOP

The East Broad Top Railroad was built in the early 1870s from a connection with the Pennsylvania Railroad at Mount Union to the east side of Broad Top Mountain. Iron ore had been mined here since the mid-eighteenth century, and smelting furnaces lined the beds of Aughwick Creek. Community names in the region, such as Rockhill Furnace, reflect its iron-producing heritage.

Unlike most railroads in Pennsylvania that were built with standard gauge track—4 feet, 8.5 inches between the rails—EBT instead adopted three-foot gauge in 1872. This choice put it among the earliest American railways to use narrow gauge, which was promoted at the time as a method of significantly reducing construction costs. Narrow gauge railroads required lighter rail and shorter ties. More importantly, smaller narrow gauge trains could more easily negotiate sharp curves and steep grades, thus allowing for substantially cheaper lines in mountainous regions. During the 1870s and 1880s, narrow gauge lines were built where standard gauge lines might have been prohibitively expensive.

The East Broad Top built southward along the Aughwick Creek. By August 1873, its tracks reached 11 miles from Mount Union to Orbisonia, the location of Rockhill Furnace. In order to tap the Broad Top coal fields, EBT pushed farther south and passed through villages at Three Springs and Saltillo before embarking on a steep, sinuous ascent into the mountains. This included boring an 830-foot curved tunnel through Sideling Hill. From here, the railroad dropped down into Coles Valley, then ascended an even steeper grade, before boring beneath Wray's Hill in a 1,235-foot tunnel. Beyond that, tracks hugged along Trough Creek and climbed to Robertsdale. Robertsdale is 30 miles south of Mount Union and the location of an important coal mine tapped in October 1874.

In 1891, East Broad Top extended its main line south to Woodvale, and ultimately its tracks reached Alvan, 33 miles from Mount Union. The railroad reached its peak in 1916—also the year

Facing page: Timeless scenes such as this make East Broad Top among the most compelling railroads in Pennsylvania. Two generations gaze in wonder at old No. 15, built by Baldwin for the railroad way back in 1914. Old, but not worn out, this locomotive has had a full life hauling coal for more than 40 years and entertaining visitors for another 50 years. Scott R. Snell

Above: A visit to East Broad Top's three-foot gauge line is a step back in time. On a clear autumn morning, EBT Mikado No. 15 simmers at Rockhill Furnace. East Broad Top is more than a typical excursion line—it's a national treasure that has preserved the essence and spirit of small-time early twentieth-century railroading. Scott R. Snell

Under the veil of a thick fog, the sounds and scents of steam railroading are even more vivid. EBT No. 12, a Mikado known as Millie, rests under steam at Rockhill Furnace. More than just a few locomotives escaped oblivion when Nick Kovalchick bought the railroad for scrap back in 1956. He saved the railroad's shops, its tracks, and cars, which have survived to the present. The railroad was an antique in its heyday, as evident by stub switches and minimal cinder ballast on its tracks. Today it's truly a relic of another age. Brian Solomon

railway trackage peaked nationally. EBT built its offices, shops, a roundhouse, and a yard at Rockhill Furnace near Orbisonia. At Mount Union, it had a relatively large yard featuring a coal-cleaning facility near its interchange with the PRR.

During its formative years, East Broad Top's operations provided an integral link for iron production in the region. In addition to hauling ore from local mines, it moved coking coal to online ovens used in the production of iron products. While delivering iron to the PRR at Mount Union, some Broad Top coal was transferred to the PRR for further transport. In addition to ore and coal, EBT also hauled ganister rock, timber, bricks, and merchandise freight. The railroad also operated a regular passenger service.

Iron traffic declined in the 1890s and dwindled away by World War I. Compensating for the loss of iron traffic was a surge in coal business. In 1926, coal accounted for about 80 percent of EBT's freight traffic. Times would never be as good as this again. By the late 1920s, output from the region's coal mines was in decline.

With the onset of the Great Depression and growing automobile ownership and road construction, EBT's passenger ridership had dropped off by the early 1930s. With this decline came scaled-back passenger operations, which only provided a daily mixed train—a train that carried both freight cars and passenger cars.

By the early 1950s, further contraction in the regional coal business pushed EBT into the red. Passenger service ended in 1954, and a year later the coal tapped out. The railroad was left with only freight movements of ganister stone, which was not enough to subsist on. The railroad operated its last common carrier revenue train in April 1956. A month later, the Kovalchick Salvage Company bought the whole line for scrap, including its rolling stock and structures. Fortunately, unlike the New York, Ontario & Western—the Old & Weary—that suffered a similar fate a year later, EBT found a happier future.

Preservation and Revival

At a time when railroads were in decline, and every year more and more lines were closing and services were

On this autumn day in 1997, time has stood still. A stub switch is rare enough in the modern world, but EBT has an even rarer three-way stub switch. (Modern switches use points.) This image at Rockhill Furnace could have been made 80 years ago. Brian Solomon

being curtailed, the loss of the East Broad Top was just the latest in a growing list of railroad casualties. Thankfully, Nick Kovalchick of the Kovalchick Scrap Company recognized the historic value of the East Broad Top and refrained from scrapping the line. After several years of EBT inactivity, Kovalchick restarted a portion of the route north of Orbisonia as an excursion line. Steam trains had been gone just long enough for curiosity and nostalgia about them to take hold.

Over the years, the railroad's historic reputation has infused a new generation of interest in the line. As of this writing in 2007, the railroad, including its shops, yards, locomotives, and cars were the property of the Kovalchick family. However, the sale of EBT was under discussion.

Visiting EBT

About 3.5 miles of the EBT line from Rockhill Furnace north to Colgate Grove is in service for seasonal week-end passenger excursions from June through October. Both first- and second-class accommodation is available. The railroad's operational highlight is its annual Fall Spectacular, held at the end of the operating season in

EBT Mikado No. 17 negotiates the yard trackage at Rockhill Furnace on a cold autumn morning. This locomotive is slightly heavier than Mikado's No. 12, 14, and 15, and as a result it has only been used infrequently in modern times. As of 2007, it was out of service. Like the other Mikados, it was built by Baldwin in Philadelphia. It has resided on EBT since its construction in 1918. Brian Solomon

October. This is traditionally when just about any equipment safe to move is brought out for service or display.

Although it was closed down in 1956, EBT was anything but a modern railroad when it ended operations, so its offices, roundhouse, and shops at Orbisonia/Rockhill Furnace survive as one of the best preserved examples of a small-town turn-of-the-century steam railroad facility in North America. However, much of the line lies derelict; it is preserved in a sense, but not restored. In places, trees more than 40 feet tall grow between the rails. The tunnels at Sideling and Wray's Hills still have tracks through them, but these tracks have not seen service in more than 50 years.

Despite many changes in the surrounding area, the old EBT around Orbisonia has retained its classic appearance. In fact, EBT largely works with authentic equipment that has been with the railroad since it was a commercial, coal-hauling operation. Although there are some facilities provided for visitors, there is minimal interference from modern and unnecessary tourist accommodations. This factor distinguishes EBT from a host of tourist railways and museums that sacrifice historical authenticity for public convenience. As a result, the EBT is one of the finest authentic railroad experiences in North America.

In addition to facilities and locomotives at Orbisonia, vestiges of the railroad's narrow gauge can be seen in a number of locations. The intrepid explorer may find remnants of the yards and facilities in Mount Union. Nearby, a standard gauge 0-6-0 used by the railroad to interchange with the PRR resides in the old engine house—its boiler has been cold since the end of freight operations. Perhaps of greater interest to the casual visitor is the old EBT station at Robertsdale, which has been restored and operated as an EBT museum by the volunteer group, Friends of the East Broad Top.

While several of EBT's vintage Baldwins have continued to ply the rails between Rockhill Furnace and Colgate Grove, two have been sequestered in this old roundhouse for more than 50 years. Nos. 16 and 18 are seen in the left and center stalls, while old No. 12, Millie, is on the right. Gems such as these, tucked away and waiting for their day in the sun to come again, have given an air of mystery and hope to EBT. Will these locomotives some day breathe steam again and march up the grade toward Robertsdale? Or will the whole of EBT fade silently into the earth, saved only for a couple of generations, but not truly preserved for all time? Scott R. Snell

Traditionally, EBT has concluded its excursion season with an annual event called the Fall Spectacular. During this event, EBT drags out everything that will run and makes a weekend of it. On this crisp autumn day, EBT's vintage Mikados are readied for the day's activities at Rockhill Furnace. Brian Solomon

East Broad Top can be reached via car by taking exit 180 (Fort Littleton) off the Pennsylvania Turnpike. Follow Route 522 north to Orbisonia. At the traffic light, take a left onto Route 994 across the Blacklog Creek. Within a couple tenths of a mile, you will see the Orbisonia station on your right and the roundhouse and shops on your left. For parking, you may turn left toward the shops and roundhouse, or turn right onto Iron Street and then take another right into another lot.

Shade Gap Electric Railway

Adjacent to EBT's facilities at Rockhill Furnace in Orbisonia is the Rockhill Trolley Museum, which operates short excursions on the Shade Gap Electric Railway using restored period trolley cars. Shade Gap branch has its own special history as EBT's oddest extension. It was extended under the name of the Shade Gap Railroad to reach the fabled South Pennsylvania Railroad. It was built in the early 1880s through rugged terrain by New York Central and Philadelphia Reading interests in an effort to compete with the Pennsylvania Railroad.

The South Penn, in conjunction with Philadelphia & Reading and Central Railroad of New Jersey, would have created a through route from the New York metro area to Pittsburgh, somewhat south of and parallel to

PRR's Main Line. Much of the South Penn was graded, including long tunnels bored through the mountains, but efforts at completing the line were aborted when J. P. Morgan stepped in and persuaded New York Central to give up the project in exchange for the West Shore Railroad. That line was being built by interests aligned with PRR to compete with Central's main line in New York State. Today, part of the South Penn route is used by the Pennsylvania Turnpike, a highway often used by visitors to EBT.

Since the South Penn aborted construction in 1885 before EBT could reach it, the branch only extended to a mine near Shade Gap, although it was pushed farther later. Traffic on this line faded before the rest of the railroad; much of it was already gone by 1956. Although it once had narrow gauge track, the line had standard gauge track installed over a short section of the branch in the 1960s to operate the trolley line. There is a little bit of dual gauge track in place where EBT and the trolleys share the wye used to turn narrow gauge steam trains.

The trolley museum claims to be the oldest of its kind in Pennsylvania, and it has restored a variety of period electric cars. In addition to trolleys, it also has several third-rail electric cars that once operated on the Philadelphia & Western/Red Arrow Lines route to Norristown.

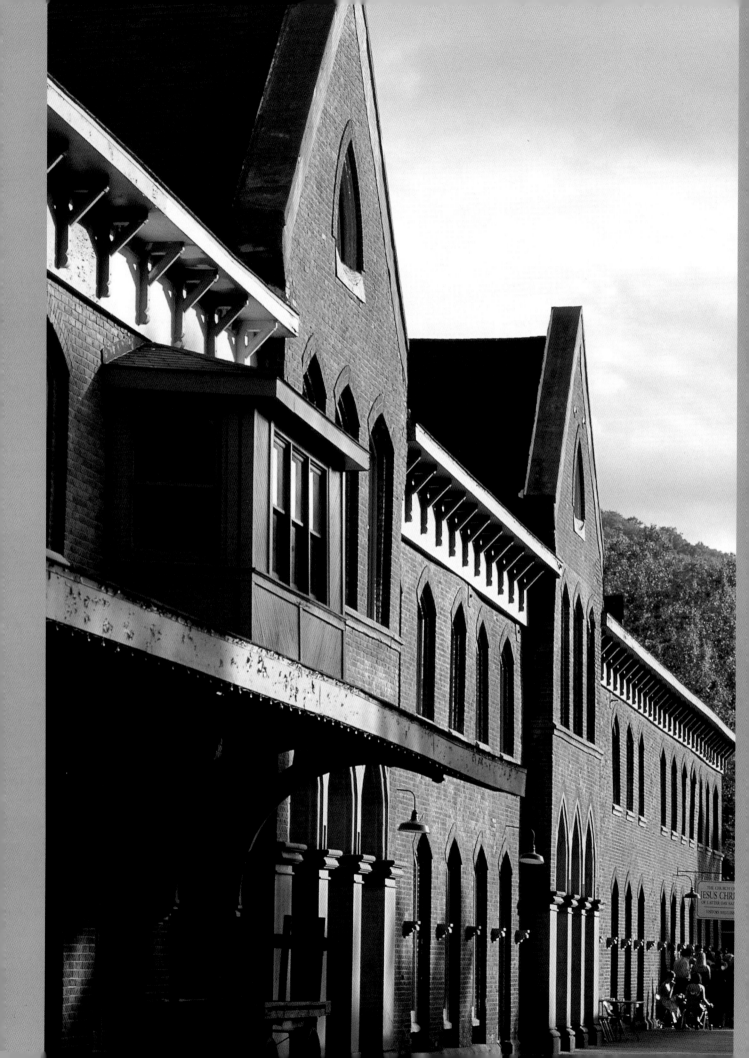

CHAPTER 14

THE ERIE RAILROAD AND THE STARRUCCA VIADUCT

The New York and Erie Railroad was conceived to connect the lower Hudson Valley at Piermont with Lake Erie at Dunkirk, New York. While its 1832 charter required that the railroad remain entirely within the state of New York, geography dictated otherwise. At a number of points, the railroad's main line was built through parts of Pennsylvania.

The route over Gulf Summit was among the Erie builders' greatest challenges.

Once cresting the summit, it dips into Pennsylvania at Lanesboro, where it spans the valley of Starrucca Creek on the magnificent stone-arch bridge known as the Starrucca Viaduct. Completed on November 23, 1848, Starrucca's 17 solid graceful arches were made from locally quarried blue stone limestone. At its highest point, the bridge is 100 feet above the valley floor. It also is 1,040 feet long.

When the railroad reached its first western terminus at Dunkirk in 1851, it was the longest continuous railroad in the United States operated by one company. Erie grew into an important east-west freight hauler. Like the other trunk lines, it gradually extended lines westward. In 1883, it leased the Atlantic & Great Western—a railroad scheme originally envisioned to connect New York, Philadelphia, and Cincinnati. This line made for a logical western extension and brought Erie from Salamanca in western New York though northwestern Pennsylvania to Marion, Ohio. Through A&GW lines, Erie tapped lucrative oil traffic in northwestern Pennsylvania, and it built yards and shops in Meadville, about 90 miles north of Pittsburgh.

Ultimately, the railroad reached Chicago. It extended other lines as well, including a main line to Buffalo and lines extending southward from its trunk

Facing page: Just a few miles west of the Starrucca Viaduct, Susquehanna, Pennsylvania, was once the location of important shops and yards. It was also a division point and a helper base for freights climbing toward Gulf Summit. Although freight trains still pass infrequently through here, they have little reason for pausing. Built in 1865 in a Victorian Gothic style, Erie's immense Susquehanna depot—known as the Starrucca House—served as hotel and a railroad eatery. Trains would pause at the depot to allow passengers a hasty meal before continuing on their journey. The building has been renovated, and it again serves as a restaurant. Brian Solomon

Above: In July 1970, an Erie Lackawanna mixed freight works westward across the Mill Rift Bridge over the Delaware River to cross from New York State into Pennsylvania. In the lead is a powerful SD45 diesel-electric. The old Erie Railroad had always been a busy freight line, which was a trend that continued under the combined Erie Lackawanna. Although some freight still flows along the Delaware, these tracks are much quieter now, as the majority of freight is routed over other lines. George W. Kowanski

into Pennsylvania coal country. One of these left the main from a junction at the west end of Starrucca and ran southward to tap the anthracite fields. Erie shared this line with Delaware & Hudson. For many years, D&H's trains operated beneath the viaduct on their way to and from yards in Carbondale, Scranton, and Wilkes-Barre via Ararat Summit. Conveyed to D&H in the mid-1950s, portions of this line were last used in 1985; most were abandoned as far as Carbondale.

Oddly, Erie's engineers selected a broad track gauge (six feet) when first constructing its line. They insisted this track would give the line greater stability and allow larger cars and locomotives to use it. The advantages of their vision proved illusory. By the 1880s, Erie was forced to regauge to the 4-foot, 8.5-inch standard track gauge.

A few miles west of Starrucca at Susquehanna, Erie established locomotive shops, servicing facilities, and yards. It also opened its famous Starrucca House hotel and restaurant. This place was an important division point on the railroad where crews and locomotives were exchanged. In the days before dining cars, Erie's passenger trains paused at the Starrucca House and allowed passengers to dine briefly in the large neo-Gothic dinning hall. Restored in the 1990s, this building again serves as a restaurant, though today's meals are served at a more leisurely pace.

The shops and yards here were phased out following the Erie Lackawanna merger of 1960. After the merger, the former Erie line over Starrucca gradually declined in importance as a through-freight route. Passenger service ended prior to Amtrak. The bridge still stands majestically over the valley, but as of 2007, it is just used a few times a week for freights operated by an affiliate of the New York, Susquehanna & Western. West of Binghamton, New York, to Buffalo, the old Erie line remains busier and serves as Norfolk Southern's freight-only main line.

Visiting Starrucca House

To visit the Starrucca House, exit Interstate 81 at Great Bend (between Scranton and Binghamton). Take Route 171 east to Oakland and go south on Route 92 across the Susquehanna River. For more information about the restaurant's hours and menu, call 570-853-3080.

Erie Railroad's most memorable and enduring landmark is its famous Starrucca Viaduct, located in northeastern Pennsylvania in the village of Lanesboro. This sunrise view was made from the hillside on the southeast side of the bridge. At one time, Delaware & Hudson's tracks passed below the bridge and up the valley to the left. Brian Solomon

BESSEMER & LAKE ERIE By Patrick Yough

For many years, the Bessemer & Lake Erie was the only major north-south line in Pennsylvania that was not owned by a large east-west trunk line. B&LE can track its origins to October 1869, with the formation of its predecessor, Shenango & Allegheny.

In 1896, steel-magnate Andrew Carnegie became involved with the line following a three-way agreement between the S&A successor, Pittsburg [sic], Shenango & Lake Erie (PS&LE), the Union Railroad, and Carnegie Steel to build a railroad from Butler to East Pittsburgh. This new railroad would connect with the Union Railroad and was organized as the Butler & Pittsburg [sic]. Its chief engineer, F. E. House, was later honored with a station named Houseville near the present-day village of Ivywood.

In January 1897, as the Butler & Pittsburg was under construction, it merged with PS&LE to form the Pittsburg, Bessemer & Lake Erie. Carnegie Steel purchased the majority of the stock in the new line, which opened on October 27, 1897. On December 31, 1900, the name was shortened to the Bessemer & Lake Erie, a line often simply referred to as the Bessemer, or by its initials.

By backing the line, Carnegie aimed to break what he saw was an anti-competitive stranglehold on Pittsburgh held by the Pennsylvania Railroad. This strategy resulted in his control of both railroads and lake shipping, which enabled Carnegie Steel to become a completely integrated operation from mine to consumer. Once the extension to East Pittsburgh was completed, the B&LE became an integral cog in Carnegie's steel-making enterprises. Iron ore mined in Minnesota's Mesabi Range was shipped by rail to Duluth or Two Harbors, where it was loaded into Carnegie-owned boats for shipment to Conneaut, Ohio. There, it was reloaded into rail cars for final transport to Carnegie's steel works in the greater Pittsburgh area. The day the first ship left Duluth for Conneaut, Pennsylvania, Carnegie wrote to his employee Henry C. Frick, noting that "today, Pittsburgh becomes a lake port."

Mineral traffic was B&LE's life blood, while passenger service was never very important. B&LE provided a round trip each way out from its hub at Greenville, Pennsylvania. The last scheduled passenger trains operated on March 5, 1955.

The Bessemer and other railroads remained important links in the Carnegie and U.S. Steel empires until 1988. At that time, a management-led buyout formed Transtar to assume ownership of all remaining U.S. Steel subsidiary railroads, as well as its Great Lake Fleet. In 2004, Transtar sold B&LE, plus sister railroad Duluth, Missabe & Iron Range and the former USS Great Lakes Fleet, to Canadian National. This seemed to make sense since DM&IR connected with CN's subsidiary Duluth, Winnipeg & Pacific. However, B&LE had no connections with the CN and has remained an isolated operation.

B&LE accomplished a few significant American railroad firsts. In 1908, the railroad received the first all-steel boxcar (built by Standard Steel Car), and it was the first railroad to use steel crossties.

The B&LE preserved two steam locomotives: 2-8-0 Consolidation Type No. 154 and B&LE's 2-10-4 Texas Type No. 643. The first, built in 1910, resides at the Henry Ford Museum in Michigan and was once the heaviest and most powerful locomotive in the world. B&LE's 2-10-4 Texas Type No. 643 resides at a little-known place in the Pittsburgh area. Although partially restored, it now faces an uncertain future.

A southbound Bessemer & Lake Erie ore train rolls past Calvin Yard near Butler on the day after Christmas. The train is en route from the Pittsburgh & Conneaut Dock at Conneaut, Ohio, to U.S. Steel's Mon Valley Works in Braddock, Pennsylvania. At North Bessemer, the train will be interchanged to the Union Railroad for delivery to the mill. For most of the last century, all of the companies involved in bringing goods from the dock to the mill were once part of the U.S. Steel Corporation. Today, the P&C Dock and the Bessemer are subsidiaries of Canadian National, while the Union RR is part of a holding company named Transtar. Patrick Yough

CHAPTER 15

BALTIMORE & OHIO

In 1827, the B&O railroad was chartered to build from the port of Baltimore, Maryland, to the Ohio River as a response to the opening of the Erie Canal. While the Delaware & Hudson and other early railroads were envisioned as industrial inhouse lines, Baltimore & Ohio was the first American railroad chartered and built as a common carrier, with traffic open to all.

The first section of line, 14 miles between Baltimore and Ellicotts Mills, Maryland, opened in May 1830 and provided daily horse-drawn passenger service. After years of slow progress, the B&O finally reached the Ohio River at Wheeling, West Virginia (then still part of Virginia), in 1852. From an early date, the B&O had envisioned a line to Pittsburgh, but was foiled for decades by Pennsylvania interests that didn't want to see the flow of freight directed to Baltimore. Despite these problems, B&O finally reached Pittsburgh in 1871 when it assumed control of the recently completed Pittsburgh & Connellsville. Having made it this far, B&O extended its reach across Ohio and Indiana, and connected to Chicago by 1874. This route, rather than its original line, developed as its primary through trunk line and put it in a good position to compete for freight and passenger business. Still, it lagged behind the nation's two largest railroads—the Pennsylvania and New York Central.

B&O also extended a main line northeast from Baltimore to Philadelphia, and with connections via the Reading and Central Railroad of New Jersey, it tapped the New York metro area. During the Panic of 1893, B&O's finances faltered, and it entered receivership in 1896. By 1900, B&O was controlled by PRR. Under the few years of PRR control, B&O improved its freight-hauling capacity, which included the construction of enormous new yards at Connellsville and New Castle, Pennsylvania. Federal anti-trust litigation separated PRR and B&O in the first decade of the twentieth century.

Facing page: The morning sun graces the old Baltimore & Ohio station at Washington, Pennsylvania. This is one of several well-maintained historic railroad structures in town. Brian Solomon

Above: In 1956, Baltimore & Ohio still had steam locomotives based at its Connellsville terminal. Here, in the gloom of night at the Connellsville roundhouse, expert photographer Jim Shaughnessy posed two locomotives that were each adorned with B&O's famous capitol dome logo. Within three years, the fires would be dumped forever, and B&O would be all diesel. Jim Shaughnessy

In the late 1920s, when railroad consolidation was being discussed nationally, B&O made two significant line acquisitions that conveniently tied in with its visions of assembling a super east-west main line across central Pennsylvania. In 1930, it bought the Buffalo, Rochester & Pittsburgh, and in 1932, it bought the Buffalo & Susquehanna. Both were coal-hauling lines serving the northwestern portion of the commonwealth.

B&O's grand plans died in the Great Depression, but the BR&P lines remained part of its system until the 1980s. Genesee & Wyoming's Buffalo & Pittsburgh has operated freight service on the Pennsylvania portion of the old BR&P since 1988. B&O trimmed much of the B&S lines in the steam era. The eastern portion was run by a colorful short line called the Wellsville, Addison & Galeton into the mid-1970s, but has since been abandoned.

In common with other northeastern carriers, the Baltimore & Ohio suffered from declining traffic and revenues after World War II. To survive in the evolving economy, B&O merged with Chesapeake & Ohio in the 1960s. B&O's lines are now a key component to CSX's eastern freight network. Amtrak's *Capitol Limited* provides daily passenger service between Washington, D.C., and Chicago via Pittsburgh over former B&O lines in Pennsylvania. CSX's former B&O line crosses the Alleghenies at Sand Patch near Meyersdale, Pennsylvania. The tortuous east slope of Sand Patch follows Wills Creek through rugged and pastoral scenery, which has long made it a popular place to photograph heavy freight trains at work.

Above: Baltimore & Ohio was in transition at Connellsville, Pennsylvania, on July 1, 1956: Electro-Motive F7 diesels had assumed most road freight assignments, yet a few old steam locomotives, such as 0-8-0 switcher 678, were still working for the railroad. In the distance is a Reading Company coal hopper. Jim Shaughnessy

Facing page: The old Baltimore & Ohio Sand Patch grade over the Alleghenies presents a daily struggle for westward CSX freight trains. These trains must ascend a brutal and sinuous grade that hugs Wills Creek on the way up to Sand Patch Tunnel at the summit near Meyersdale. Here, an eastward manifest train has a rolling meet with a westward intermodal train clawing its way up through the Falls Cut Tunnel. This is the route of Amtrak's daily Capitol Limited, *which connects Washington and Chicago via Pittsburgh.* Brian Solomon

Right: On January 23, 1947, a Baltimore & Ohio passenger local on the old Buffalo & Susquehanna departs Galeton, Pennsylvania, bound for Addison, New York. W. A. Lucas collection, Railroad Museum of Pennsylvania PHMC

CHAPTER 16

DIVERSE RAILROADS, MUSEUMS, SITES, AND EXCURSIONS

The wide scope and breadth of Pennsylvania railways enabled builders in the nineteenth century to push lines to virtually every corner of the state. In addition to the dense network of common carriers were an array of industrial and coal lines, logging railroads, interurban electrics,

streetcars, and funicular lines. Although greatly scaled back from its peak, Pennsylvania's railway lines remain vital to its economy. The historic and recreational railway heritage can be discovered and enjoyed in many communities.

Many towns have preserved structures, locomotives, and other railroad equipment for display. Others have museums dedicated to the railroad's heritage in the Keystone State.

Pennsylvania Trolley Museum

One of the best run railway museums in Pennsylvania, and one of the oldest, is the Pennsylvania Trolley Museum. It is located about 45 minutes southwest

of Pittsburgh near Washington, Pennsylvania. This museum began in the 1950s as an effort to preserve the heritage and equipment of Pennsylvania's then rapidly disappearing street railway and interurban lines. The current site was selected in 1953 when Pittsburgh Railways abandoned its interurban route to Washington. Interestingly, three of the preserved cars were operated to the site under their own power before the old tracks were lifted.

Today, the museum captures the atmosphere and essence of a classic Pennsylvania electric railway. It operates more than two miles of line—some of which is built adjacent to the old Pittsburgh Railways line to Washington and runs parallel to a former Pennsylvania Railroad branch that is now operated weekdays to serve local freight customers by the Pittsburgh & Ohio Central. Part of the line utilizes an old PRR branch that ran to the nearby Arden Mines.

Facing page: The Pennsylvania Trolley Museum is one of the best re-created electric railways in the commonwealth. Its well-maintained line is among the few preserved railways equipped with an authentic operating signal system. It uses vintage Union Switch & Signal color light hardware. Like locomotive builder Baldwin, trolley car manufacturer Brill, and freight car builder American Car & Foundry, railroad equipment supplier US&S was based in Pennsylvania and sold its products around the world. Here, Philadelphia & West Chester Traction Company car No. 78 splits a set of vintage US&S signals. Brian Solomon

Above: Pittsburgh Railways once served the streets of McKeesport southeast of downtown. The tracks are long gone, but the old trolleys that worked Route 56 are fondly remembered in this mural along the main street. Brian Solomon

The museum once operated as the Arden Trolley Museum, which reflected its location. The present name was adopted in 1992 to better reflect the museum's mission.

The museum's entire line is equipped with an operating signal system that is comprised of hardware salvaged from other lines in the Pittsburgh area. This makes it one of the few railway museums in Pennsylvania that offers a working demonstration of signaling practice. Since many Pennsylvania electric street railways were built to an unusual broad gauge, the museum's main line mainly uses this gauge instead of the common 4-foot, 8.5-inch standard. It does, however, have some standard gauge track to display heavy railroad equipment and allow for interchange.

The museum collection is largely stored in car barns, which protect the cars from the elements and aid in restoration. Most of the collection comes from regional electric railways, including operations in Philadelphia, Johnstown, and Pittsburgh. Several beautifully restored trolleys are regularly operated for visitors. These trolleys represent many different eras and come complete with vintage seating and advertising. Car barn tours are available during most operating sessions.

In addition to electric trolleys, the museum has a vintage horsecar that operated in the streets of Pittsburgh as early as the 1870s and several significant pieces of heavy railroad equipment. Locomotive B73 is a rare diesel-electric built by Westinghouse and Baldwin in 1930. It is among the oldest surviving diesel locomotives, and it is believed to be the oldest operable diesel-electric in the United States. Also in the collection are two cabooses, one of which is from the Monongahela. The other was originally New York, Ontario & Western, and after 1953, it belonged to the coal-hauling Unity Railways.

Johnstown was the last small city in Pennsylvania to operate its own electric streetcar network. On December 27, 1958, Johnstown Traction Company car No. 350 works the Ferndale Line near the Stonycreek Bridge and the crossing with the Baltimore & Ohio's branch to Johnstown. When it ended service less than two years after this photo, JTC spanned 27 route miles. Although little remains of Johnstown's trolley lines, car No. 350 has been preserved at the Pennsylvania Trolley Museum near Washington. Richard Jay Solomon

The museum is located a few miles north of Washington, and it is easily reached from Interstate 79. Days and hours of operation vary depending on the season.

The city of Washington also has several historic railroad structures. Two of these are from the old three-foot-gauge Waynesburg & Washington line, which was later operated by PRR. They include the distinctively ornate passenger station on South Main Street and a beautifully renovated 1884 PRR freight house that is used to house offices of several local businesses on Washington Street near Chestnut Street. The other rail site in town is the restored former Baltimore & Ohio passenger station. Built in 1892, it is now occupied by the Washington County Tourism Promotion Agency.

More Rewarding Railway Sites

In Pennsylvania's northwest corner, east of Erie and along the old Water Level Route—operated as a busy CSX east-west freight corridor that hosts Amtrak's New York–Chicago *Lake Shore Limited*—the town of North East is home to the Lake Shore Railway Historical Society Museum. Based at the restored Lake Shore & Michigan Central passenger station built in 1899, the museum displays a variety of equipment, including locomotives manufactured by General Electric at Erie. This museum is in part a tribute to GE, America's oldest major locomotive manufacturer and currently the leading producer of modern diesel-electric locomotives.

In the Juniata Valley, The Huntingdon County Transportation Society has preserved the old Hunt signal tower along the former PRR Main Line just west of the Huntingdon Amtrak station. When the tower is open, its second floor is a great place to watch Norfolk Southern freights roll up and down the valley. Nearby is the old PRR station, partially restored to its Victorian appearance in the 1990s. The station is set back from the tracks and reflects an earlier PRR alignment through town.

At Latrobe, Pennsylvania, portions of the old PRR station have been reinvented as a railroad-theme restaurant called DiSalvo's Station. Its upscale Italian menu may be enjoyed as Norfolk Southern trains thunder by overhead. An old passenger car has been incorporated as part of the dining room. Railroad photographs and art are displayed on the walls, and in the bar railroad heralds are incorporated in the tables. Amtrak's daily *Pennsylvanian* stops at the station platform above the restaurant.

Pittsburgh once had an intensive network of city streetcar lines. At 3 P.M. on July 9, 1958, Pittsburgh Railways PCC car No. 1128 pauses at Diamond Street in downtown. Although PAT now operates a modern light-rail network, most of the old Pittsburgh Railways street trackage is a memory. A few of the historic cars can be viewed at the Pennsylvania Trolley Museum. Richard Jay Solomon

Philadelphia Transportation Company No. 2711 is a classic Presidents' Conference Committee (PCC) car that was built during the 1940s. SEPTA still assigns similar cars to its No. 15 route on Girard Avenue, while this car and its sister 2723 reside at the Pennsylvania Trolley Museum. On this autumn afternoon, 2711 is serving as the "birthday trolley"—a popular theme attraction that enables a family to charter a vintage streetcar for a child's birthday. In place of the traditional destination sign is the child's age and name. Once introduced to railroading, a child may remain an enthusiast for life. Brian Solomon

PENNSYLVANIA'S VISUAL HERITAGE By John Gruber

Pennsylvania railroads have a strong visual heritage, often on view at museums across the state. That heritage ranges from the serious pioneering photography commissioned for the Pennsylvania Railroad to whimsical illustrations of Phoebe Snow riding on the Lackawanna's Road of Anthracite, with loads of commercial and calendar art thrown into the creative mix. One early daguerreotype—one of railroading's rare early images—shows the locomotive Tioga and its crew in front of a hotel in Philadelphia on the Philadelphia & Columbia Railroad in about 1849.

Before 1900, when Philadelphia was the photography center of the United States, the Pennsylvania Railroad sent out some of the best photographers from its headquarters to record scenic attractions along its line. A few of the prominent photographers, listed below, show the diversity of the work.

The PRR designated William T. Purviance (1829–1905) as its official photographer in 1867. He maintained studios in Philadelphia and Pittsburgh, and he marketed his work under such titles as *Purviance's Views on the Pennsylvania Central Railroad* and *Scenery of the Pennsylvania Railroad*. He also traveled on the Erie and Lehigh Valley.

Frederick Gutekunst (1831—1911) had a prominent role in the photography exhibitions at the 1876 Philadelphia Centennial Exposition. He was responsible for large landscape views along the Pennsylvania Railroad.

William H. Rau (1855—1920) was the most prominent of all of them. Although best known for his landscape views for the World's Columbian Exposition in Chicago in 1893, Rau and his studio produced negatives for the Pennsy from 1887 to 1924. Rau covered the Lehigh Valley in 1895 and again in the 1910s. *Traveling the Pennsylvania Railroad: Photographs of William H. Rau,* edited by John C. Van Horne with Eileen E. Drelick (2002), attests to Rau's importance. The Rau PRR photographs are on long-term deposit at the Library Company of Philadelphia. Modern 8x10-inch copy prints of the collection are available for researchers to study at the library.

The Southern Alleghenies Museum of Art at Altoona frequently exhibits Rau photographs from the Altoona Area Public Library Collection. "William H. Rau's photographs demonstrate the importance of the railroad in the development of Western Pennsylvania culture and industry," said Barbara Hollander, SAMA-Altoona coordinator.

In addition to lines already profiled, the state has several other passenger excursion services. The historic city of Gettysburg enjoys a variety of themed weekend trips provided by the Pioneer Lines Scenic Railway over a Gettysburg Railroad former Reading Company line. The Bellefonte Historical Railroad provides occasional excursions with vintage Budd Company RDCs on the Nittany & Bald Eagle's former PRR Bald Eagle branch, which connects Tyrone and Lock Haven. Southwest of

Philadelphia, the West Chester Railroad offers 90-minute excursions on a former Pennsylvania Railroad branch; these trips run seasonally on weekends, on selected holidays, and by charter.

Some of the most interesting and unusual excursions are privately organized, infrequent events. Philadelphia-based Juniata Terminal Company owns a variety of historic diesel locomotives and passenger cars, providing them for occasional special trips over lines in

William N. Jennings (1860–1946), a PRR office worker in Philadelphia, initially traveled on his company pass for photographic trips. He opened a studio in 1900 and continued making photographs for the railroad into the 1930s. Other PRR rail photographers from the 1930s include Robert Dudley Smith (1897–1972), a Philadelphia chemist, and Elizabeth R. Hibbs (1905–1993), who exhibited photos of children at the *Parents' Magazine* gallery in New York City.

The list of notable photographers for other lines includes William Henry Jackson, the famed photographer of the West, who traveled for the Baltimore & Ohio in the 1890s and for the Lackawanna in 1899.

For calendar artists, the leader is Grif Teller (1899–1993), who painted calendars and posters for the PRR. *Crossroads of Commerce* by Dan Cupper (1992) has all the details about Teller, who worked as an artist in calendar production and ad specialties for the Osborne Company. From 1928 to 1942 and from 1947 to 1958, he created the oil paintings used on the Pennsylvania Railroad's annual advertising calendars that are distributed worldwide. In the 1970s, Teller received commissions to paint railroad scenes, mostly of the Pennsylvania Railroad. In October 1984, the Railroad Museum of Pennsylvania displayed his paintings as its first major art show. Many of Teller's works are still on display, along with a re-creation of his studio. The Commonwealth of Pennsylvania's railroad heritage license plate, unveiled at the museum in December 1998, features Teller's famous 1928 painting *When the Broad Way Meets the Dawn*, set along Juniata River Valley in central Pennsylvania in the late 1920s.

Harry Stacey Benton (1887–1947) used photographs as his inspiration for painting the colorful car cards for which the Lackawanna Railroad is known. Their rhyming jingles, named for Phoebe Snow in 1903 by Earnest Elmo Calkins, caused a sensation. When Marion Murray, a photographer's model posing as "the maid all in white," came to Binghamton, New York, in 1904, a crowd of 10,000 people turned out to greet her. She modeled for the railroad until 1907 and then popped up dressed in uniform in World II and introduced a streamlined train in 1949. She died in 1967.

Often museums are seen as the way to preserve significant pieces of railroad equipment, but without photographs, drawings, sketches, patent drawings, advertisements, posters, broadsides, postcards, labels, and a host of other printed railroad memorabilia, the artifacts would remain ill-comprehended. It takes four kinds of records—artifacts, paper records, pictorial records, and oral histories—to interpret the full story of our railroad heritage.

Pennsylvania and across the region. Among Juniata Terminal's most significant equipment is a pair of restored former Pennsylvania Railroad E8As dressed in classic Tuscan red and looking much the way they would have in the 1950s. Other past trips have operated from Altoona around the Horseshoe Curve; from Harrisburg to Renovo via Norfolk Southern's normally freight-only former Northern Central and Philadelphia & Erie route via Sunbury; and over Amtrak's former PRR lines. Reading & Northern's passenger department provides occasional excursions over the railroad's normally freight-only lines. R&N owns a variety of historic steam and diesel locomotives, which can make for colorful excursion consists.

Pennsylvania's railway network continues to evolve. As traffic changes, some lines are closed, converted to biking trails, or allowed to return to nature. Other lines, long disused, occasionally find new life. A short line might reopen a branch that was discontinued by a larger

Latrobe, Pennsylvania, once the home of Rolling Rock beer, is among the few lucky towns in western Pennsylvania still served by Amtrak. While passengers may board the Pennsylvanian *at track level, the old railroad station has been adapted into a trendy railroad-themed restaurant. The classic old station is seen under a rising moon in the historic downtown. Brian Solomon*

railroad, and from time to time a museum or tourist railway will reopen lines that were long abandoned. Still, the wise visitor should take nothing for granted. An old steam locomotive, long stored, may be restored to service, but likewise, that locomotive will only have a limited lifespan before it requires rebuilding again—a costly, time-consuming job. Main lines that are busy with traffic today may change in time. An excursion service operating today may be discontinued tomorrow. Changes in local economies, floods, fires, as well as petty disputes between squabbling operators, have doomed more than one preserved railway. Take the time to explore, experience, and enjoy Pennsylvania's rich railway heritage that remains. There really is no time like the present.

Below: General Electric DASH9-40CW diesels built in Erie lead a Norfolk Southern unit coal train eastward past the restored Hunt Tower—located just west of the Amtrak station in Huntingdon, Pennsylvania. Brian Solomon

APPENDIX

ANTHRACITE COUNTRY

Jim Thorpe, Pennsylvania, Switchback Gravity Railroad
34 miles north of Allentown, Pennsylvania, off Interstate 476
Website: www.visitjimthorpe.com

Pioneer Tunnel Coal Mine
19th and Oak streets
Ashland, Pennsylvania 17921
Phone: 570-875-3850
Website: www.pioneertunnel.com

Steamtown
150 South Washington Avenue
Scranton, Pennsylvania 18503-2018
Phone: (888) 693-9391
Website: www.nps.gov/stea/

Tunkhannock Viaduct and Martins Creek Viaduct
Tunkhannock Viaduct is off U.S. Highway 11 south of Nicholson, Pennsylvania. Martins Creek Viaduct is off of State Route 547, near Kingsley, Pennsylvania, which is 11 miles north of Nicholson on U.S. Highway 11.

Wayne County Historical Society Museum and Wayne County Chamber of Commerce
810 Main Street
Honesdale, Pennsylvania 18431
Phone: (570)253-3240
Website: www.waynehistorypa.org

PHILADELPHIA AND PENNSYLVANIA DUTCH COUNTRY

30th Street Station
2955 Market Street
Philadelphia, PA 19104-2989

Middletown & Hummelstown Railroad
136 Brown Street
Middletown, Pennsylvania 17057
Phone: (717) 944-4435
Website: www.mhrailroad.com

New Hope & Ivyland Railroad
32 West Bridge Street
New Hope, Pennsylvania 18938
Phone: (215) 862-2332
Website: www.newhoperailroad.com

Railroad Museum of Pennsylvania
300 Gap Road
Ronks, Pennsylvania 17572

Reading Terminal Train Shed (now part of the Pennsylvania Convention Center)
12th and Arch streets
Philadelphia, Pennsylvania 19107

Strasburg Rail Road
301 Gap Road
Ronks, Pennsylvania 17572
Phone: 717-687-7522
Website: www.strasburgrailroad.com

Suburban Station
1617 John F. Kennedy Boulevard
Philadelphia, Pennsylvania 19103

Wanamaker, Kempton & Southern Railroad
42 Community Center Drive
Kempton, Pennsylvania 19529-0024
Phone: 610-756-6469
Website: www.kemptontrain.com

THROUGH THE MOUNTAINS VIA THE HORSESHOE CURVE

Allegheny Portage Railroad National Historic Site
110 Federal Park Road
Gallitzin, Pennsylvania 16641
Phone: (814) 886-6150
Website: www.nps.gov/alpo/

Altoona Railroaders Memorial Museum
1300 Ninth Avenue
Altoona, Pennsylvania 16602
Phone: (814) 946-0834
Website: www.railroadcity.com

Cassandra, Pennsylvania, Railfan Welcome Center
22 miles northeast of Johnstown, Pennsylvania, off State Route 53

Cresson, Pennsylvania, train viewing park
31 miles northeast of Johnstown, Pennsylvania, off U.S. Highway 22

Gallitzin, Pennsylvania
34 miles northeast of Johnstown, Pennsylvania, off State Route 53

Horseshoe Curve
Kittaning Point Road
Altoona, Pennsylvania 16602
Phone: (814) 941-7960
Website: www.railroadcity.com/hc/index.php

Johnstown, Pennsylvania, historic funicular railway
67 miles east off Pittsburgh, off U.S. Highway 22 and State Route 56

RAILWAYS LARGE AND SMALL

Bellefonte Historical Railroad
320 West High Street
Bellefonte, Pennsylvania 16823-1304
Phone: 814-355-2917
Website: www.bellefontetrain.com

DiSalvo's Station
325 McKinley Avenue
Latrobe, Pennsylvania 15650
Phone: 724.539.0500
Website: disalvosrestaurant.com

Duquesne Incline
1220 Grandview Avenue
Pittsburgh, Pennsylvania 15211-1204
Phone: 412-381-1665
Website: incline.pghfree.net

East Broad Top Railroad
Orbisonia, Pennsylvania 17243
Phone: (814)-447-3011
Website: www.ebtrr.com

Hunt signal and former Huntington PRR station
500 Allegheny Street
Huntington, Pennsylvania 16852
Phone: 814-643-6308
Website: /users.lazerlink.net/~dalew/index.html

Lake Shore Railway Historical Society Museum
31 Wall Street at Robinson
North East, Pennsylvania 16428-0571
Phone: 814-725-1911
Website: www.velocity.net/~lsrhs/index.html

Monongahela Incline
East Carson St.
Pittsburgh, Pennsylvania 15211
Phone: (412) 361-0873

Pioneer Lines Scenic Railway
106 N. Washington Street
Gettysburg, Pennsylvania 17325
Phone: (717) 334-6932
Website: /www.gettysburgrail.com

Pennsylvania Trolley Museum
1 Museum Road
Washington, Pennsylvania 15301
Phone: 724-228-9256
Website: www.pa-trolley.org

Pine Creek Rail-Trail
Phone: (570) 724-2868
Website: www.gis.dcnr.state.pa.us/railtrails/

Rockhill Trolley Museum
430 Meadow Street
Rockhill Furnace, Pennsylvania 17249
Phone: 814-447-9576
Website: www.rockhilltrolley.org

Starrucca Viaduct and Starrucca House
504 Front Street
Susquehanna, PA 18847
Phone: (570) 853-3080
Website: www.starruccahouse.net/

Station Square
100 West Station Square Drive
Pittsburgh, PA 15219
Phone: 800-859-8959
Website: http://www.stationsquare.com/main.asp

Tioga Central Railroad
577 Hills Creek Road
Wellsboro Junction, Pennsylvania 16901
Phone: (570) 724-0990
Website: www.tiogacentral.com

West Chester Railroad
200 E. Market Street
West Chester, Pennsylvania 19382
Phone: 610-430-2233
Website: westchesterrr.com

BIBLIOGRAPHY

BOOKS

1846–1896: Fiftieth Anniversary of the Incorporation of the Pennsylvania Railroad Company. Philadelphia: Pennsylvania Railroad Company, 1896.

A Century of Progress: History of the Delaware and Hudson Company 1823–1923. Albany, NY: Delaware & Hudson, 1925.

All Stations: A Journey Through 150 years of Railway History. London: Thames and Hudson, 1978.

Ahrons, E. L. *The British Steam Railway Locomotive 1825–1925.* London: Bracken Books, 1926.

Alexander, Edwin P. *The Pennsylvania Railroad: A Pictorial History.* First Ed. New York: W. W. Norton, 1947.

Anderson, Elaine. *The Central Railroad of New Jersey's First 100 Years.* Easton, PA: Center for Canal History and Technology, 1984.

Apelt, Brian. *The Corporation: A Centennial Biography of United States Steel Corporation, 1901–2001.* Pittsburgh: Cathedral Publishing, University of Pittsburgh, 2000.

Archer, Robert F. *A History of the Lehigh Valley Railroad: Route of the Black Diamond.* Berkeley, CA: Howell-North Books, 1977.

Beaver, Roy C. *Off with the Old on with the New . . . The Story of Steam Locomotives on the Bessemer and Lake Erie Railroad and Predecessor Companies.* Pittsburgh: Bessemer and Lake Erie Railroad, 1954.

——. *The Bessemer & Lake Erie Railroad, 1869–1969.* San Marino, CA: Golden West Books, 1969.

Beck, John. *Never Before in History: The Story of Scranton.* Northridge, CA: Windsor Publications, 1986.

Bezilla, Michael. *Electric Traction on the Pennsylvania Railroad 1895–1968.* State College, PA: Pennsylvania State University Press, 1981.

Binney, Marcus and David Pearce, eds. *Railway Architecture.* London: Bloomsbury Books, 1979.

Brignano, Mary and Hax McCullough. *The Search for Safety.* Pittsburgh: Union Switch & Signal Division, American Standard, 1981.

Bruce, Alfred W. *The Steam Locomotive in America.* New York: Bonanza Books, 1952.

Bryant, Keith L. Jr. *Railroads in the Age of Regulation, 1900–1980.* New York: Bonanza Books, 1988.

Burgess, George H. and Miles C. Kennedy. *Centennial History of the Pennsylvania Railroad.* Philadelphia: The Pennsylvania Railroad, 1949.

Bush, Donald J. *The Streamlined Decade.* New York: George Braziller, 1975.

Casey, Robert J. and W. A. S. Douglas. *The Lackawanna Story.* New York: McGraw-Hill, 1951.

Chernow, Ron. *The House of Morgan.* New York: The Atlantic Monthly Press, 1990.

Churella, Albert J. *From Steam to Diesel.* Princeton, NJ: Princeton University Press, 1998.

Conrad, J. David. *The Steam Locomotive Directory of North America, Vols. I & II.* Polo, IL: Transportation Trails, 1988.

Cupper, Dan. *Horseshoe Heritage: The Story of a Great Railroad Landmark.* Halifax, PA: Withers Publishing, 1996.

Curtis, Thomas, et al. *The American Railway: Its Construction, Development, Management, and Appliances.* New York: Benjamin Blom, Inc., 1972.

Daughen, Joseph R. and Peter Binzen. *The Wreck of the Penn Central.* Boston: Beard Books, 1971.

Doherty, Timothy Scott and Brian Solomon. *Conrail.* St. Paul, MN: MBI Publishing Company, 2004.

Droege, John A. *Freight Terminals and Trains.* New York: McGraw-Hill, 1912.

——. *Passenger Terminals and Trains.* New York: McGraw-Hill, 1916.

Drury, George H. *The Historical Guide to North American Railroads.* Waukesha, WI: Kalmbach Publishing Company, 1985.

——. *Guide to North American Steam Locomotives.* Waukesha, WI: Kalmbach Publishing Company, 1993.

Dubin, Arthur D. *Some Classic Trains.* Milwaukee, WI: Kalmbach Publishing Company, 1964.

——. *More Classic Trains.* Milwaukee, WI: Kalmbach Publishing Company, 1974.

Ermert, Emil R. *The Story of Pioneer Tunnel Coal Mine & Steam Train.* Privately published, 1994, 2005.

Farrington, S. Kip Jr. *Railroads at War.* New York: Coward-McCann, Inc., 1944.

——. *Railroading from the Rear End.* New York: Coward-McCann, Inc., 1946.

——. *Railroads of Today.* New York: Coward-McCann, Inc., 1949.

Ferrell, Mallory Hope. *Colorful East Broad Top.* Forest Park, IL: Heimburger House Publishing Company, 1993.

Grant, H. Roger. *Erie-Lackawanna: Death of an American Railroad.* Stanford, CA: Stanford University Press, 1994.

Greenberg, William T. Jr. and Frederick A. Kramer with Theodore F. Gleichmann Jr. *The Handsomest Trains in the World: Passenger Service on the Lehigh Valley Railroad.* Westfield, NJ: Bells & Whistles, 1978.

Greenberg, William T. Jr. and Robert F. Fischer. *The Lehigh Valley Railroad East of Mauch Chunk.* Martinsville, NJ: The Gingerbread Stop, 1997.

Grenard, Ross and Frederick A. Kramer. *East Broad Top to the Mines and Back.* Newton, NJ: Carstens Publications, 1990.

Hare, Jay V. *History of the Reading.* Philadelphia: John Henry Strock, 1966.

Harlow, Alvin F. *The Road of the Century.* New York: Creative Age Press, 1947.

Haupt, Herman. *General Theory of Bridge Construction.* First Ed. New York: Appleton, 1855.

Henwood, James N. J. *Laurel Line: An Anthracite Region Railway.* Glendale, CA: Interurban Press, 1986.

Hilton, George W. *American Narrow Gauge Railroads.* Stanford, CA: Stanford University Press, 1990.

Holton, James L. *The Reading Railroad: History of a Coal Age Empire, Vols. I & II.* Laurys Station, PA: Garrigues House, 1992.

Hungerford, Edward. *Daniel Willard Rides the Line.* New York: Van Rees Press/G. P. Putnam's Sons, 1938.

——. *Men of Erie.* New York: Random House, 1946.

Jacobs, Harry A. *The Juniata Canal and Old Portage Railroad.* Hollidaysburg, PA: Blair County Historical Society, 1941, reprinted 1997.

Keilty, Edmund. *Interurbans without Wires.* Glendale, CA: Interurban Press, 1979.

Kirkland, John F. *Dawn of the Diesel Age.* Pasadena, CA: Interurban Press, 1994.

Kobus, Ken and Jack Consoli. *The Pennsylvania Railroad's Golden Triangle: Main Line Panorama in the Pittsburgh Area.* Upper Darby, PA: The Pennsylvania Railroad Technical and Historical Society, 1998.

Lewie, Chris J. *Two Generations on the Allegheny Portage Railroad.* Shippensburg, PA: Burd Street Press, 2001.

Lyon, Peter. *To Hell in a Day Coach.* Philadelphia: Lippincott, 1968.

Marre, Louis A. *Diesel Locomotives: The First 50 Years.* Waukesha, WI: Kalmbach Publishing Company, 1995.

Marre, Louis A. and Paul K. Withers. *The Contemporary Diesel Spotter's Guide, Year 2000 Edition.* Halifax, PA: Withers Publishing, 2000.

McLean, Harold H. *Pittsburgh & Lake Erie Railroad.* San Marino, CA: Golden West Books, 1980.

Mellander, Deane E. *East Broad Top: Slim Gauge Survivor.* Silver Spring, MD: Old Line Graphics, 1995.

Middleton, William D. *When the Steam Railroads Electrified.* Milwaukee, WI: Kalmbach Publishing Company, 1974.

——. *Landmarks on the Iron Road.* Bloomington, IN: Indiana University Press, 1999.

Middleton, William D. with George M. Smerk and Roberta L. Diehl. *Encyclopedia of North American Railroads.* Bloomington, IN: Indiana University Press, 2007.

Miller, Donald L. and Richard E. Sharpless. *The Kingdom of Coal.* Philadelphia: University of Pennsylvania Press, 1985.

Moedinger, William M. *The Road to Paradise.* Privately published, 1983.

Mott, Edward Harold. *Between the Ocean and the Lakes: The Story of Erie.* New York: John S. Collins, 1900.

Pietrak, Paul V. with Joseph G. Streamer and James A. Van Brocklin. *Western New York and Pennsylvania Railway.* Hamburg, NY: Privately published, 2000.

Plowden, David. *Bridges: The Spans of North America.* New York: Norton, 1974, 2002.

Potter, Janet Greenstein. *Great American Railroad Stations.* New York: Wiley, 1996.

Pratt, Edwin A. *American Railways.* London: Macmillan and Company, 1903.

Protheroe, Ernest. *The Railways of the World.* London, 1920.

Rosenberger, Homer Tope. *The Philadelphia and Erie Railroad.* Potomac, MD: The Fox Hills Press, 1975.

Salisbury, Stephen. *No Way to Run a Railroad.* New York: McGraw-Hill Education, 1982.

Saunders, Richard Jr. *The Railroad Mergers and the Coming of Conrail.* Westport, CT: Greenwood-Heinemann Publishing, 1978.

——. *Merging Lines: American Railroads 1900–1970.* DeKalb, IL: University of Northern Illinois Press, 2001.

Saylor, Roger B. *The Railroads of Pennsylvania.* State College, PA: Pennsylvania State University, 1964.

Shaughnessy, Jim. *Delaware & Hudson.* Berkeley, CA: Howell North Books, 1967.

Shank, William H. P. E. *Vanderbilt's Folly: A History of the Pennsylvania Turnpike.* Annapolis, MD: American Canal and Transportation Center, 1993.

——. *Historic Bridges of Pennsylvania.* Annapolis, MD: American Canal and Transportation Center, 1997.

——. *Sylvester Welch's Report on the Allegheny Portage Railroad.* Gettysburg, PA: Thomas Publications, 1975.

Sinclair, Angus. *Development of the Locomotive Engine.* Cambridge, MA: MIT Press, 1970 (first edition, 1907).

Snell, J. B. *Early Railways.* London, 1972.

Solomon, Brian. *The American Steam Locomotive.* Osceola, WI: MBI Publishing Company, 1998.

——. *Railroad Stations.* New York: Metro Books, 1998.

——. *The American Diesel Locomotive.* Osceola, WI: MBI Publishing Company, 2000.

——. *Railway Masterpieces: Celebrating the World's Greatest Trains, Stations and Feats of Engineering.* Iola, WI: Krause Publications, 2002.

——. *Railroad Signaling.* St. Paul, MN: MBI Publishing Company, 2003.

Starr, John W. *One Hundred Years of American Railroading.* New York: Dodd Mead, 1928.

Staufer, Alvin F. *Pennsy Power III.* Medina, OH, 1993.

Steinman, David B. and Sara Ruth Watson. *Bridges and Their Builders.* New York: Dover Publications, 1957.

Stevens, Frank W. *The Beginnings of the New York Central Railroad.* New York: G. P. Putman, 1926.

Stilgoe, John R. *Metropolitan Corridor.* New Haven, CT: Yale University Press, 1983.

Stover, John F. *History of the Baltimore & Ohio Railroad.* West Lafayette, IN: Purdue University Press, 1987.

Taber, Thomas Townsend, III. *The Delaware, Lackawanna & Western Railroad, Vols. I & II.* Williamsport, PA: Self-published, 1980.

Talbot, F. A. *Railway Wonders of the World, Vols. 1 & 2.* London: Waverley Book Company, 1914.

Thompson, Slason. *Short History of American Railways.* Chicago: Bureau of Railway News & Statistics, 1925.

Thoms, William E. *Reprieve for the Iron Horse—the Amtrak Experiment—Its Predecessors and Prospects.* Baton Rouge, LA: Claitor's Publishing Division, 1973.

Treese, Loretta. *Railroads of Pennsylvania—Fragments of the Past in the Keystone Landscape.* Mechanicsburg, PA: Stackpole Books, 2003.

Trewman, H. F. *Electrification of Railways.* London, 1920.

Vance, James E. Jr. *The North American Railroad.* Baltimore, MD: Johns Hopkins University Press, 1995.

Waddell, J. A. L. *Bridge Engineering.* New York: John Wiley & Sons, 1916.

Walker, Mike. *Steam Powered Video's Comprehensive Railroad Atlas of North America--North East U.S.A.* Feaversham, Kent, UK: Steam Powered Publishing, 1993.

Warren, J. G. H. *A Century of Locomotive Building by Robert Stephenson & Co. 1823–1923.* Andrew Reid & Company Ltd., Newcastle upon Tyne, 1923.

Wells, Bruce P. *Pennsylvania Trolley Museum—Preserving Pennsylvania's Transit Heritage.* Washington, PA: Pennsylvania Trolley Museum, 2006.

Westing, Frederic. *Penn Station: Its Tunnels and Side Rodders.* Seattle, 1977.

Westing, Frederic and Alvin F. Staufer. *Erie Power.* Medina, OH: Alvin Staufer, 1970.

White, John H. Jr. *A History of the American Locomotive—Its Development: 1830–1880.* Baltimore, MD: John Hopkins University Press, 1968.

——. *The American Railroad Passenger Car, Vols. I & II.* Baltimore, MD: Johns Hopkins University Press, 1978.

——. *Early American Locomotives.* Toronto: Dover Publications, 1979.

White, Roy V. and A. C. Loudon. *Car Builders Dictionary.* New York: Simmons-Boardman, 1916.

Williams, Harold A. *The Western Maryland Railway Story.* Baltimore, MD: Western Maryland Railway Company, 1952.

Winchester, Clarence. *Railway Wonders of the World, Vols. 1 & 2.* London: Amalgamated Press, 1935.

Yates, John A. *Standard Specifications for Railroad & Canal Construction.* Chicago: The Railway Age Publishing Company, 1886.

Young, William S. *Starrucca: The Bridge of Stone.* Published privately, 2000.

Zimmermann, Karl R. *Erie Lackawanna East.* New York: Quadrant Press, 1975.

——. *The Remarkable GG1.* New York: Quadrant Press, 1977.

PERIODICALS

Baldwin Locomotives. Philadelphia, PA [no longer published]

CTC Board—Railroads Illustrated, Ferndale, WA.

Diesel Era, Halifax, PA.

Jane's World Railways. London.

Locomotive & Railway Preservation. Waukesha, WI [no longer published]

Official Guide to the Railways. New York.

RailNews. Waukesha, Wis. [no longer published]

Railpace Newsmagazine, Piscataway, NJ.

Railroad History, formerly *Railway and Locomotive Historical Society Bulletin.* Boston.

Railway Age, Chicago and New York.

Railway Gazette, 1870–1908. New York.

Railway Signaling. Chicago and New York. [no longer published]

Railway Signaling and Communications, formerly *The Railway Signal Engineer.*

The Railway Gazette, London.

Trains. Waukesha, WI.

Vintage Rails. Waukesha, WI. [no longer published]

BROCHURES, CATALOGUES, MANUALS, PAMPHLETS, RULE BOOKS, AND TIMETABLES

Association of American Railroads. *American Railway Signaling Principles and Practices.* New York, 1937.

CSX Transportation. *Baltimore Division, Timetable No. 2,* 1987.

Conrail. *Pittsburgh Division, System Timetable No. 5,* 1997.

Delaware, Lackawanna & Western. *A Manual of the Delaware, Lackawanna & Western,* 1928.

Erie Railroad. *Erie Railroad: Its Beginnings and Today,* 1951.

General Code of Operating Rules, Fourth Edition, 2000.

General Electric. *Dash 8 Locomotive Line.*

General Railway Signal. *Centralized Traffic Control, Type H, Class M, Coded System, Handbook 20.* Rochester, NY, 1941.

New Jersey Transit. *Lackawanna Cut-Off Passenger Rail Service Restoration Project.* Vol. 1, No. 1. 2004.

NORAC Operating Rules, 7th Edition. 2000.

Pennsylvania Railroad public timetables, 1942–1968.

Steamtown National Historic Site. *The Nation's Living Railroad Museum.*

Switchback Gravity Railroad Foundation. *The Route of the Switch Back: A Walker's Tour,* 1997.

The Wanamaker, Kempton & Southern, Inc. *A Passenger's Guide to the Train Ride from Kempton to Wanamaker.*

REPORTS AND UNPUBLISHED WORKS

Bell, Kurt R. *Roster of Historic Locomotives and Rolling Stock in the Railroad Museum of Pennsylvania Collection.* Strasburg, PA, 2002, revised 2007.

Clemensen, A. Berle. *Historic Research Study: Steamtown National Historic Site, Pennsylvania.* Denver, CO: U.S. Department of the Interior, 1988.

Chappell, Gordon. *Flanged Wheels on Steel Rails—Cars of Steamtown.* Unpublished.

McKnight, Patrick. *Mattes Street Signal Tower Historic Structure Report.* Scranton, PA: Steamtown National Historic Site, 2003.

Morgan, Mark L. and Thomas H. E. Campion. *Delaware, Lackawanna & Western Boxcar No. 43651. Historic Structure Report.* Scranton, PA: U. S. Department of the Interior, Scranton, 1996.

National Park Service. *Historic American Engineering Record: Steamtown National Historic Site, Pennsylvania.* Washington, DC: U.S. Department of the Interior, 1989.

INDEX

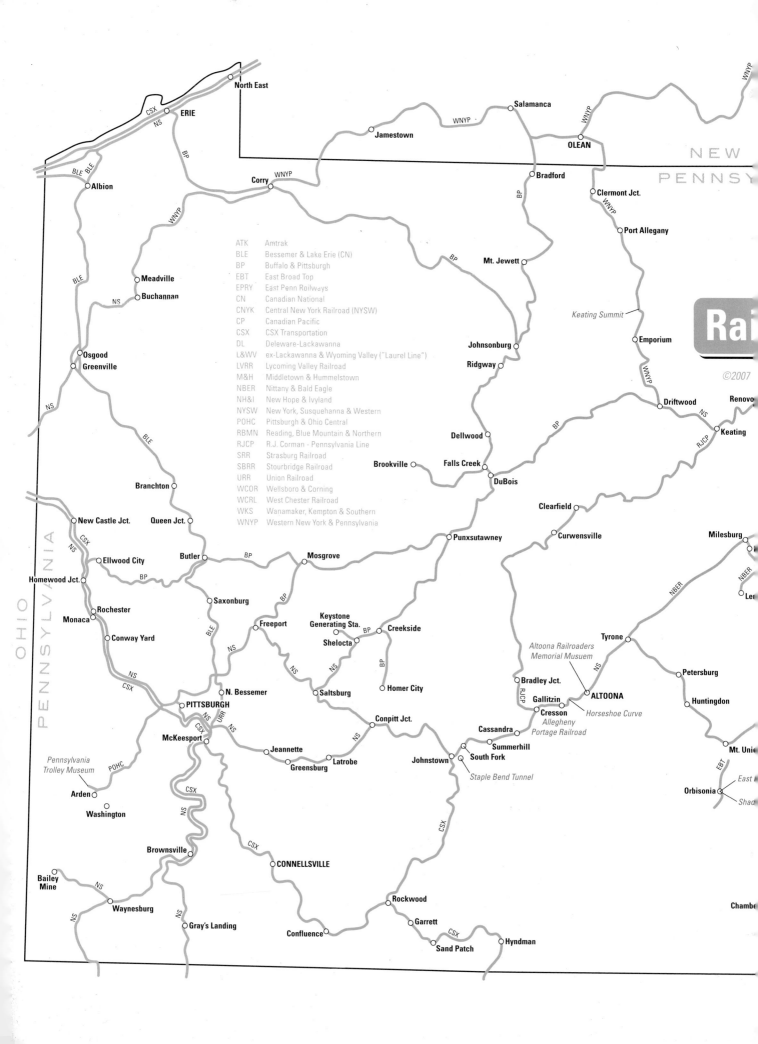